WARTIMES REMEMBERED
World War II and Korea

By Residents of Woodland Pond, New Paltz

Donald "Pete" Johnston

Managing Editor

Editors and interviewers

Halema Hassan

Paul Lurie

Anne Allbright Smith

Raymond D. Smith, Jr.

Lucille Weinstat

RESIDENTS OF WOODLAND POND, NEW PALTZ

Front cover photograph is a composite of photographs from the book, by Pete Johnston, Annette Chait Finestone, Jay Bishop and Frank Martini. The background photo: Nagasaki, Aug. 9, 1945 by Charles Levy from a B-29 Superfortress.

Unless otherwise noted, photographs are courtesy of the authors.

Published by the author residents at Woodland Pond

ISBN: 9781484805367

FIRST EDITION

Printed in the United States of America

ACKNOWLEDGEMENTS

This volume could not have been assembled without the support, encouragement, ferreting out of old photos and documents, etc. by spouses, partners, off-spring and friends of those whose stories make up the book.

Others assisted or contributed in a variety of ways:

Carol O'Biso, who was unstinting with her computer skills and support and who, having published her own book through CreateSpace, was an invaluable navigational aide through the process

Gretchen Daum, who was encouraging from the beginning, facilitated early meetings, ongoing events and publicity relating to this project

Sarah Hull, who was immediately enthusiastic and helpful with logistics

Robert E. Passanisi, Historian, Merrill's Marauders Association, who corrected errors, provided clarification and details that enhanced a story

We salute our authors, some of whom are sharing the full account of their experiences for the first time.

The Editors

GENESIS

For Christmas 2011 Anne's sister, Joan Ashley, a resident of Kendal at Hanover, NH gave us a copy of *World War II Remembered*. This is the collected experiences of residents of Kendal during World War II. Some stirring, many funny and some tiny but telling vignettes.

This was hardly the first such volume prepared but it was the first we had ever seen and it impressed both of us. The Kendal at Hanover Residents' Association had gathered, edited and self-published the book and there it was, available on Amazon. Brian Williams and NBC's "Nightly News" got wind of it and did a very short segment on the book, featuring the strong faces and voices of some of the contributors. Within a week, Amazon had sold 7,000 copies.

Like their authors, these stories are fragile. Nobody could remember or tell them but those who were there, a dying breed. They are great stories and, but for the determination of a handful of folks at Kendal, would never have seen the light of day.

Clearly there had to be many stories at Woodland Pond at New Paltz, NY, also a Continuing Care Retirement Community (CCRC), but to save them they had to be written down. Gretchen Daum, Activities Coordinator, was enthusiastic. Pete Johnston, a career writer and editor, volunteered his skills as Managing Editor and, for the May 2012 *Woodland Life*, wrote a come-on piece for an initial meeting. About fifty would-be authors turned out, stories began coming in, and others began writing their own stories. Here they are.

-Anne and Ray Smith

Photo courtesy of Gretchen Daum

Donald H. "Pete" Johnston

1924 – 2013

Pete readily volunteered his services as Managing Editor of this book. He had writing and editing experience at United Press and *The New York Times* and had taught at Columbia University's Schools of Journalism and of International and Public Affairs so he was a natural. In addition to his overall coordinating responsibilities, Pete contributed his own story as well as uncovering, writing and editing others.

When some editors kept up the pressure to get the book out, Pete observed, "I made the mistake of being casual about a retirement community and thinking that we actually were in retirement." Pete did impress on all of us: get the lead right, use dialogue, and spice the narrative. We will miss his gentleness, humility, and wry humor.

Even though he didn't live to see finished sale copies, the first, hard copy proof of this book went to Pete.

CONTENTS

MAROONED FOR 46 DAYS

Albert Becker

As told to Pete Johnston

"I was just 19 when I enlisted in the U.S. Navy and entered World War II in December, 1942. I was one of six Becker children – three boys and three girls. I was the youngest boy, a year out of high school and working as a cub reporter for a small publication in Oklahoma. I was a slow grower as a kid, and didn't sprout to full size until I reached the teens. I tried farming, but I didn't like it. Hence, the newspaper job.

"Why, then, did I decide to leave the newspaper and enlist? I felt the stories I was given were uninteresting. Mostly society and social stuff. I figured the war had bigger stories. Besides, I knew I was about to be drafted, which meant the Army, and mud and foxholes. The Navy, I figured, was a cleaner life and overall less dangerous. So I went home and enlisted—in the Navy. I was slightly underage and my father had to sign for me."

Al was right about bigger stories. His own turned out to be one of the biggest, and it attracted wide public attention in the media. He was put into the Navy Armed Guard, in which his job as a gunner was to guard and escort allied ships to Atlantic Ocean ports. This meant evading the German submarines that preyed on the many convoys that carried vital military and civilian provisions to allied forces. Al and the other gunners were responsible only for guarding the ship; running the ship was the responsibility of a second group aboard, the merchant seamen. The two contingents did not mix on board.

Al didn't have to wait long for a big story, though it wasn't the kind he was looking for. On his first voyage, in frigid December, the old freighter he and other gunners were escorting—*City of Flint*—was torpedoed and sunk. The 19-year-old from rural Iowa managed to jump clear and survive amid the burning wreckage, fierce winds, and giant waves. And with 10 other survivors he soon began a remarkable 46-day voyage marooned on a choppy ocean in an open 18 foot lifeboat. Only one of the survivors failed to hold on through the whole ordeal.

Was Albert, the young Navy gunner, scared after the *City of Flint* was sunk from under him and he was left struggling in the ocean? "No, I wasn't," he replies emphatically. "I was mad as hell!!!"

City of Flint had been scheduled to join a convoy bound for Gibraltar with supplies for the troops in North Africa. Her holds were packed with gasoline, which made the more experienced crewmen nervous.

Earlier, the convoy ran into a battering winter sea, which tossed ships out of formation. *City of Flint* lasted just under 10 days before she was forced out of the convoy. Watch duty became an ordeal because trouble could come from all four sides. "We had a cargo of telephone poles on deck and they'd begun to break loose—we were losing them and leaving a trail behind us." However, with everyone pitching in, the ship's deck was secured and *City of Flint* was able to move ahead to return to the convoy in a couple of days.

Then, as recounted by Al: "It was just sunset, which is the most dangerous time because it's very hard to adjust to the darkness. All eyes were on the water. I was on the poop deck with the 5 inch gun, and that's when we heard that there was a torpedo coming. The fellas up in the bow hollered over the phones and you could see the wake, the phosphorescence on the surface of the water. The ship lurched trying to miss it, but we were too slow and it didn't miss. There was a big boom— we were hit right where we had the gasoline in the number one and the number two holds. As it exploded, the ship ripped the bridge right off. There was fire on the water that lit things up, and you could see the telegraph poles going up in the air and coming down into the sea like matchsticks. At first the engines were moving the ship forward—past crew members, your buddies hollering—who had already jumped into the sea. You knew you were going by them but there was nothing you could do.

"There was a lot of fuel on the water, patches of it. You tried to get it away from you so it wouldn't burn you, but it stuck to you. It got hotter than hell, and you struggled to keep it from burning your face or your clothes. I could see from the flames that there was nothing but telegraph poles, and you can't last long in the water with nothing to get on to. Then I saw a rope ladder on the ship and I scrambled back on deck again. The only fire aft was caused by the gasoline that sprayed back from the explosion; the canvas and rope were burning, but the ship was not on fire there. My buddy, Steve Kubik, was on deck, and we decided to get the big plank raft down in the water."

From the life raft Al watched the stern of *City of Flint* lift out of the sea, the screws still turning and, with a great hiss of steam, disappear. At that juncture they saw a lifeboat emerge from the smoke. "They spotted our raft and asked if we wanted to get in with them since they had only nine men. We took the food from the raft and got in, and that's when we ran into this machine gun fire. We figured the sub had to be firing. It was going right over our heads. I surmised they were going to make a good job of it, and do everybody in. We got the heck out of that boat and into the water, and we stayed there until things quieted down."

The U-boat had quickly torpedoed *City of Flint* apparently without seeing Al and his companions. The U-boat did some shooting, but the target was unclear because of the darkness and smoke. Nevertheless, the gunfire would later have a serious effect on Al and his group. They rowed all night to get away, and later feared that may have been a mistake. They learned that the other lifeboats stuck together and were picked up three days later.

"The next morning we took inventory of the 18 foot lifeboat. Its rudder was lost, but a mast, canvas, and a little rope remained. Emergency provisions included about 30 cans of pemmican (a concentrate of meat and fruit extract packed into a container the size of a sardine can), malted milk tablets, and 15 gallons of water. We divided the food and water to ensure they would last for three weeks, feeling sure we would be rescued by then. Water was the most important item, and it had to be preserved, protected, and carefully rationed."

"The food in the pemmican can," Al explains, "would come out as a slug. You would take your knife and each man got a quarter of a can. Then each man got two malted milk tablets and a container of water about the size of a shotgun shell. The rations were distributed twice a day, mid morning and late afternoon. Everyone took his share and nobody tried to get more."

Without communications, the survivors quickly lost contact with their families and rescuers. "My parents thought I was gone, and made funeral arrangements."

There was no recognized hierarchy of authority or rank, at least for the first few weeks of the marooning. The prevailing attitude was that "we're all in this together and we have to stick together." The two different groups, the five merchant seamen and the six Navy personnel, growled occasionally at each other's behavior, but always quieted down and returned to their respective ends of the boat. The Navy bunch had implied authority. "We had the government-assigned .45 revolver so we let them know that we were going to man the boat and wanted all the help we could get.

"A critical source of help was a seaman named Rohmar Johansan, a Norwegian who had demonstrated skills above all others about sailing an open boat. He became the navigator and put together a sail and rudder. The Navy boys were relieved to find someone who knew what he was doing and helped.

"All differences were ignored as everyone struggled to stay alive when a punishing storm struck. First the clouds formed, then the waves got choppy, then the swells, and then those 40 foot waves. And you're right in them in this little boat...The boat rolled like a cork. We headed into the wind and thanked God we had the Norwegian. The men were bailing water constantly with the two army helmets that were on board, and they took turns holding the rudder, a chore that almost pulled off their arms. They were left drenched, exhausted, and extremely cold. At night they would huddle together and share the warmth of each other's bodies.

"One of the merchant seamen obviously couldn't take it anymore. Mentally he had lost it. He'd lay out his money in the boat, dry it, and give a five dollar bill to someone and tell him to go call a water taxi. He'd want somebody to go out and buy him a bucket of crabs. We worried about him, but we had to be careful with him because he picked up a hatchet and he'd never let go of it.

"Then we were hit by another rough storm, and we were all immersed in our usual battle against the storm's effects. It was then that the guy with the hatchet jumped out of the boat. We never saw him again. He just decided that he'd had it.

"After three weeks of their hazardous journey, the survivors found it hard to keep up their spirits, and the loss of this man was another blow to the morale in the lifeboat. I recall that, unless a storm was hitting us, the men would not move about. They would sit in one place for hours on end. Our regular break was to read a copy of the New Testament, two or three times a day, weather permitting. It settled your mind, gave you something to look forward to. The Bible was circulated too, and every reading would start with the 23rd Psalm. 'The Lord is my shepherd…Yea though I walk through the valley of the shadow of Death, I will fear no evil, for thou art with me.'"

Despite the challenging circumstances, Al and his remaining companions didn't give up hope of being rescued. They knew every day how long they'd been fighting German subs and the Atlantic. At dawn each day a man at the helm would put a scratch on the boat's side. By this system the group knew that within three weeks they had sighted their first ship, and rescue seemed possible at last.

"But it didn't happen. We waved vigorously and hollered with all our might. We even fired a few flares, but the ship either didn't see us or didn't want to pay us any attention. That was a heartbreaker. Some of the guys cried.

"About this time, less than three weeks out, it became clear that the rations would not last. We kept cutting back, but that wasn't good enough. So we had to add, and it was fish. To oversee stricter control of the rationing, I was put in charge of food for men in the boat. I willingly accepted because someone had to do it, and the assignment indicated that the men accepted and trusted me.

"The first catch in the fishing initiative was a barracuda. We couldn't kill him because we were afraid we might punch a hole in the bottom of the boat. So we waited most of the day for that sucker to die. He was bouncing all over the boat, but he made us a banquet. You took the skin off it and cut up the meat. It was raw fish but it tasted like steak. Afterwards we felt guilty because we ate too much at once. Any fish we caught later we rationed like the rest of the food. There were sharks and pilot fish, and they looked pretty easy to catch. When the sharks swam near the boat, those pilot fish came real close. We took out our sheath knives and we would just punch them in the belly and throw them in the boat. You probably missed fifty of them before you got one."

A month passed and Al and his Navy guardsmen were still confident they would be rescued. They believed that you don't quit if you have an ounce of strength and if you're all pulling together. There were a few encouraging signs to support that theory. The weather improved, and the color of the sea changed. Seagulls started to follow the boat and seaweed drifted past them. These factors, Rohmar Johansan assured them, indicated that they were nearing land.

At dawn on March 12, 1943, the men in the lifeboat saw the plane. At first it looked like a big seagull. But the men in the plane waved—and then the plane disappeared. Hours later, at dusk, smoke from the destroyer HMS *Quadrant* appeared on the horizon. The survivors were too weak to assist their rescuers. "We were one hell of a mess, unshaven, our hair a foot long, shirts white from salt, and all very emotional."

All of the men suffered from saltwater boils and dehydration, and some had minor injuries to their arms and legs caused by knocking about during the many storms. But the 10 survivors escaped serious injury and were in good basic condition, given the rough conditions they faced for 46 days.

"The survivors journeyed from Gibraltar to the United States on a fast troopship. Their families had not expected to see them again, so the reunions were happily emotional. At first my thoughts turned regularly to the sailboat. I'd dream about the storms because they scared the hell out of me. Now the memory of it returns only at difficult times, but as a comfort."

After Al Becker was rescued from 46 days on the Atlantic in a small lifeboat, he was assigned to easier Navy work in New York City. He organized and maintained office equipment such as addressographs until 1960. The next year he moved to Poughkeepsie to work for IBM as a quality engineer. Al retired in 1991 and "became a homebody watching the family grow." He and Cathy have one son, one daughter, four grandchildren, and five great grandchildren. The Beckers joined Woodland Pond in January, 2013.

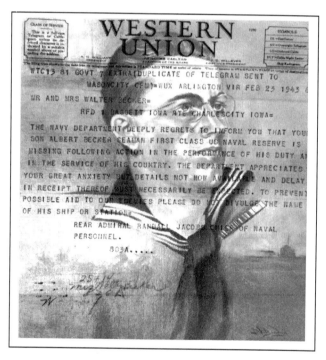

BAIL-OUT!

Jay Bishop

Curtiss C-46, photo courtesy of Martin McGuire

In the spring of 1952 at Brady Air Force Base near Fukuoka, Japan, two Curtiss Commando C-46 troop transport aircraft were involved in a taxiing accident. One airplane crashed into another, causing considerable damage to both planes. The right engine and wing of one was severely damaged, as was the tail section of the other. Fortunately no one was injured and it was reported that repairs could save one of the two aircraft. Late that summer the *Far East Stars and Stripes* newspaper had a big article praising the maintenance crew at Brady AFB in using the undamaged parts of both aircraft to rebuild and render flyable one badly needed transport. This aircraft was to be put back into service, flying the round robin courier flights connecting the many small airbases in Korea with Brady, in Japan.

In late October, 1952 I was stationed aboard an Air Force sixty-three foot Crash Rescue Boat based off the end of the runway at a Marine Air Base in Pohang, Korea. This is where we waited, on standby, in case one of the jet fighters happened to crash into the ocean. (This was before the advent of rescue helicopters!) Our home base was back on the docks in Fukuoka and so, on a regular basis, one of the crew would hop on a courier flight back to Japan to pick up mail or repairs or the like. This time it was my turn to make the trip.

After picking up our mail and supplies I wended my way back to Brady AFB to catch my flight back to Korea. It was a miserable, rainy morning; the flight office told me and four other passengers that it would be a couple of hours before the weather was expected to clear. We went over to the NCO club to wait it out. Three hours and several beers later we were told it would still be some time before we could leave. Another couple of beers and they finally said we were going to fly despite the weather. The five of us were really not feeling much pain as we boarded our plane. We and a cargo of boxes were the only passengers and the pilot, copilot and radio operator were the crew.

The aircraft took off into the rain clouds and we bounced along in the turbulence for about an hour. The radio operator and the five of us were standing under the only heat duct in the cargo area of the plane, trying to keep warm. The radio operator told us how we were privileged to be flying on such a famous plane, the one that had been written up in the *Stars and Stripes*!

All of a sudden there was a big drop in altitude as we hit an air pocket. Then, a screeching sound as a large crack appeared in the side of the fuselage. The radio operator raced up front and came back shouting that we had to bail-out! I don't remember much after that except that I was dangling in a chute in the night sky, getting very wet in the rain, and then I sank up to my knees in something very soft, wet and smelly. I was in a rice paddy! In retrospect that was probably good because I landed stiff-legged and could have broken one or both of my legs. Those of you who know anything about Asian rice paddies will know why it was so smelly!

Fortunately I was not far from a main road and a GI in a military truck picked me up and drove me to a nearby army base. (We drove with the windows open!) I understand that the C-46 continued west for several miles before it came down on one of the many Korean mountains.

REMEMBER THE WAR TIME SCRAP DRIVES?

Jay Bishop

1936 Plymouth with WW II
bumpers 1943

1936 Plymouth with proper bumpers
1945

On December 7, 1941 I was eight years old and in the fourth grade at Worthington Hooker School in New Haven, Connecticut. My father was an economics instructor at Yale. The attack at Pearl Harbor seemed far away, but soon came the nightly east coast blackouts and my father's air-raid warden duties. So, in the summer of 1942 my father loaded my mother, my two sisters and me into our 1936 Plymouth, with our precious "A" rationed gas, and headed west to a new position of assistant professor at Oberlin College in Ohio.

Oberlin was a new experience for all of us. My father, a dyed-in-the-wool

Englishman, got into the war effort in a big way. He was very concerned about his father, who was living on the south coast of England, and tried to do everything possible to bring an end to the war. We were big into rationing, scrapping anything metal for the war effort, victory gardens and the like.

In 1943 my father got the bright idea that the front and rear bumpers on our '36 Plymouth were very good, heavy steel. He went to the lumber yard and bought two nice long 2 x 4's and painted them a sort of yellowy cream color. Then he removed the bumpers from the car and took the bumpers over to the special container for war effort scrap metal. He then installed the 2 x 4's on our car. A reporter from the *Cleveland Plain Dealer* newspaper came, wrote a nice article, took pictures of the scrap container as well as the '36 Plymouth, and my father became a sort of local hero.

The war continued, the navy V-12 unit continued to drill in the street right outside our bedroom windows, and in mid-1945 the war in Europe was over. My father's job at Oberlin was over as well and the time came for us to move back to the east coast, so my father decided to see if he could replace the steel bumpers for the car. He went down to Axelrod's, the local junkyard, and found two beautiful 1936 Plymouth bumpers, complete with the marks he had made when removing them for the scrap drive. So much for the Oberlin war effort!

Jay Bishop and his wife, Faye, have been residents at Woodland Pond since the end of September, 2009. They moved here from Somers, New York, in Westchester County, where they had lived (on and off) for 35 years. Jay was born in London, England and immigrated to the U.S. in 1938. With his father, a college teacher at Yale and Oberlin, he spent his growing years in Connecticut and Ohio. At seventeen he enlisted in the U.S. Air Force, just as the Korean War began. He spent the next four years stationed in various locations in Japan and Korea, winding up in Greenville, South Carolina.

After the Air Force he spent eight years with the insurance arm of General Motors, followed by fifteen years in Credit Risk Management with the finance subsidiary of Ford Motor Company. This was followed by twenty one years in Risk Management with Citibank. Part of the Citibank experience included five years of living overseas, two and a half years in Australia and then two and a half in Korea. As a traveling man he has worked, at least a few days each, in 43 states and about 40 different countries.

Now retired for more than fourteen years, Jay has served as Treasurer of the Presbytery of Hudson River, where he is now a member of their Board of Trustees.

SAVING ART

Paul O. Bleecker, U. S. Army

As remembered by his wife, Madeleine

Paul Bleecker landed in Italy around 1944 and ended up in Florence, where he was transferred to the Monuments, Fine Arts and Archives section under the Civil Affairs and Military Government. These units were established in 1943 to assist in the protection and restitution of cultural property in war areas. Thirteen nations and approximately 345 men and women participated in this effort during and after the war.

In Paul's unit there was an Englishman, a Swiss, Paul and perhaps one other. His office was in the Uffizi Gallery, whose origins go back to the sixteenth century. Among Paul's chores was signing – in triplicate – the documents required to initiate, with war continuing, the repair and restoration of monuments.

He was instrumental also in the restoration of museum art that had been hidden in farm houses and places underground, and among those Paul met in his work were the historian and critic, Bernard Berenson, and the art historian and eventually director of the Ca' d'Oro Museum, Michelangelo Muraro.

Already an accomplished violinist, Paul made friends with other musicians, learned to speak Italian and joined a group of chamber musicians. It was a relatively peaceful, creative war experience, the kind that is not often dwelt on but well worth remembering.

Born in 1921, Paul had completed a year of college when he joined the Army in 1942. After his discharge he got his law degree from Columbia University in 1947, attended law school in Paris and met and married Madeleine there. On their return to New York, Paul practiced commercial law in New York City where his fluency in Spanish, Italian and French helped his international practice. He and Madeleine lived in Little Neck, NY and Paul played in the Great Neck Philharmonic Orchestra.

After his death in 1987, Madeleine began dividing her time between a Dutch style barn she owns in Stone Ridge, NY and a condo in Puerto Rico. She came to Woodland Pond in 2010.

A FARM LAD AT SEA

Warren Church

Sailing the difficult waters of the North Atlantic in the winter and the extensive expanse of the Pacific were certainly life changing for a teenager who grew up on a dairy farm in St. Johnsbury, Vermont.

I was 14 years old when Pearl Harbor occurred. As part of a tight-knit community, with families who had lived in St. Johnsbury for generations, we all got caught up in supporting the war effort. Mostly, we were involved in collecting scrap iron and searching for seeds of milk pods that were used for the stuffing in life preservers. At age 17 I had all of the seasonal chores that a young boy growing up on a farm would have:

milking, plowing, planting, maple sugaring, etc., but I was anxious to do something for our country so I left high school in my junior year and enlisted at the Coast Guard Station #1 in Boston, Massachusetts. Going to Boston was quite an adventure, and about 20 of us "young kids" were sworn in on June 13, 1945.

Boot camp was at Manhattan Beach, Brooklyn. When we arrived we were issued our duffle bags and our new clothes. Thirty of us trained at the same time and we stuck together. My first new experience was being taken along with all of the new recruits to the nearby Merchant Marine swimming pool. The instructor ordered all of the non-swimmers to the far side of the pool, and the swimmers to the near side. I knew that if you could not swim it would mean extra time in training, so I took a chance and jumped into the swimmer's side. Whew! I made it — an experience I would not soon forget. They had some other challenges for us including going through a mock gas chamber, as well as many other tests of survival.

Since it was near the end of the war we were allowed to go to New York City. I learned that I could ride the subway into New York for 5 cents and go anywhere in the system on the same nickel. I saw where the plane crashed into the Empire State Building (2/28/45) and experienced V-J Victory night in Times Square. I also went to the "Pepsi-Cola Canteen" and got tickets to several Broadway shows. Another highlight was seeing Jack Dempsey, Heavyweight Boxing Champ, doing exercises near our camp. What exciting adventures for a Vermont country teen.

On October 24, 1945 I went on board the USS *Admiral W. L. Capps* in Newport News, Virginia. This was basically a ship building port but during wartime it was used as a staging area for military personnel. I was on the ship's sixth voyage. The ship made a total of ten voyages as the USS *Admiral W.L. Capps* before being decommissioned in May of 1946 at the marine terminal in Bayonne, N.J. The ship had been built by Bethlehem Steel in Alameda, California, and had seen action in the Pacific Theater. Just before I went on board the ship's armaments were removed so I did not see the ship in her original form. I was assigned to watch duty in the Food Refrigeration Equipment Room. The ship had to store enough food to feed 5,000 returning troops and crew for about ten days.

The location of my watch, which was 4 hours on and 8 hours off, was on the lowest deck of the ship, just above the bilge. During severe storms I would look at the rivets on the side of my station and wonder what would happen if those rivets should fail, but I did not dwell on that thought. My first voyage was on November 3, 1945 to LeHavre, France. Although we had a good trip over I was not prepared for the devastation that I witnessed as we approached. There were live mines floating in the harbor, as the battles of D-Day had totally destroyed the harbor. It was challenging for the crew to tie the boat to parts of the pier that remained so that the returning troops could board. On our return trip we experienced rough waters in the North Atlantic; the trip was so difficult that the ship's captain had to slow down and change course for awhile to ease the stress on the ship. As we approached Newport News, Virginia, I thought of the song, "I saw the harbor lights" because, as the Harbor Master guided the ship into port, I could see the lights, decorations, and hundreds of people waiting to greet the returning troops. It was colorful, emotional and thrilling.

After we offloaded the troops we took on supplies – food, and fuel for our next trip, which was to Marseilles, France. Again, we found total devastation, huge ships "belly up" and vast debris everywhere. We loaded about 5,000 returning troops, heading for Newport News. We went via the Straits of Gibraltar; I had never seen such blue water as that of the Mediterranean. We arrived in Virginia just before Christmas of 1945, and four days later received orders to pick up 4,700 more soldiers from Yokosuka, Japan. We stopped at Pearl Harbor to pick up more materials; the destruction caused by the 1941 attack had been cleared up by then. Usually a calm ocean, we seemed to have been sucked into some type of hole in the Pacific, and the ocean came over the bow of the ship — some 70 or 80 feet – a frightening experience, to say the least.

We made one trip from San Francisco to Okinawa for troop rotation, and in April of 1946 we sailed from San Francisco to Manila, Philippines to pick up American civilians who had been held in a Japanese prison camp at Santo Tomas. There were parents and children, as well as injured soldiers -- many in terrible conditions; one man was so sick that he died on board and was buried at sea. We brought the passengers back to Pearl Harbor for immigration and processing and then sailed to San Francisco. The date was April 12, 1946 – the same day that FDR died. We normally think of the North Atlantic as being rough in the winter, but it was not bad compared to the North Pacific in the winter. Our return trip from Okinawa to San Francisco via the northern route was the roughest ride I ever took. All items that were not tied down were shaken out of position. After that experience, it was clear sailing.

During these trips I stood watch in the machine room and at one time I was on the midnight to 4a.m. watch (the watches varied on a regular schedule). I was in the machine room where I monitored data on the temperatures in the food lockers. On one evening an officer came in. He looked around and approved the way things were running under my watch. He was the ship's captain, and I was pleased to have the approval of someone of that caliber.

On my last trip the ship was directed back to New York City via the Panama Canal; it was quite an adventure to see the locks. I received an Honorable Discharge on May 9, 1946, and returned to Vermont to finish my senior year of high school.

I learned that the ship was then decommissioned, returned to the Maritime Commission and transferred to the US Army. The ship was subsequently refitted, made into an army transport ship, and used during the Korean and Vietnam wars. It was once again transferred to the Navy and was renamed the *USNS General Hugh J. Gaffey*. The transport was sunk during military exercises as a missile target in 2000. It was a rewarding and memorable time at sea for a Vermont country boy.

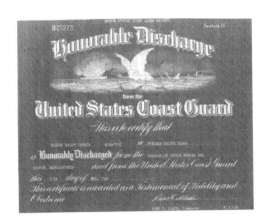

After leaving the service Warren completed high school and attended Michigan State College where he earned a BS in Dairy Science and an MS in Agricultural Engineering. He and his wife, Barbara, moved to Poughkeepsie in 1964 where Warren accepted a position with Delaval Separator Co., a manufacturer of industrial food processing equipment. He designed plate heat exchangers used for the pasteurization of dairy products. Later in his career he designed fuel oil purification systems used in power plants; this work took him to Saudi Arabia, Indonesia and Chile.

Interviewer: Halema Hassan

THE FARM

Marilyn Coffey

The Farm at time of purchase, 1948

The isolated white farmhouse sat nestled in the mowed meadow, surrounded by deep woods and a shallow stream on the eastern border. It was near Yaphank, Long Island out near the Hamptons at the eastern end where the soil is dark and rich enough to grow the finest crops.

It was the winter of 1942 and, while the war against Germany continued, my father Thomas Clarke, a captain in the U.S. Army who was home awaiting deployment to Africa and my uncle, George Hendrickson, were renovating the farm which the two families had purchased as a weekend retreat.

While Yaphank was far from the fighting, the town was the home of two different camps that housed prisoners of war: Camp Siegfried, a Bund or center for a German-American heritage group which claimed to be both pro-Nazi and Pro-American, and Camp Upton, an American military camp. Camp Upton's internment program combined civilians imprisoned as a result of the alien enemy control program as well as enemy combatants. Security at Camp Upton was strict and escape attempts were punishable by shooting.

The simple two story house that Tom and George were renovating had a neglected appearance, crying out for a coat of paint and repair to the shutters that hung limply from the windows. Each bedroom included a chamber pot for the convenience of those wishing to avoid a nighttime trip to the outhouse.

Ancient newspapers excavated from the walls opened during the recent renovations spoke of the Civil War. Articles of special interest about President Lincoln and the Union troops were framed and hung over the big creek stone fireplace which anchored the south end of the living room where the family gathered in the evenings to share stories.

The house and parcel of land, known to us as "the farm", was surrounded by the much larger working farm owned and managed by the Schuster clan. The Schuster's farm was a short walk from our farm and was an endless source of adventure for children raised in Brooklyn. Their large family provided an array of children to play with, as well as the security of good neighbors and the use of their telephone in emergencies.

On a bitter winter day George and Tom worked in the dining room at the back of the house, paneling the walls with knotty pine boards. The dining room's ample windows overlooked the stream that ambled through the back of the property. Only sparsely shielded by the recent growth of small trees and brush, the barren winter landscape left the stream visible from the house.

Suddenly Tom's attention was drawn beyond the window toward the stream as he became aware of something moving in the woods. He and

George were supposed to be alone. He quickly jumped to his feet and spotted two men dressed in the garb of POWs making their way down the stream towards the Bund.

Tom grabbed George and pointed, drawing attention to the two men moving on their property. The brothers-in-law were instantly aware that they needed to set a plan in action. Seeing the old musket above the fireplace that had long served nothing more than decorative purposes, the two men stealthily but courageously stole into the woods where they easily overcame two wet, shaking and bitterly cold prisoners. With gestures to accommodate for the language barrier and the threat of the ancient, yet unloaded gun, the prisoners were escorted back to the farmhouse.

Not until Tom and George entered their house did the condition of the two escaped prisoners become apparent – that the prisoners had escaped without shoes on their feet or even a jacket on their backs. Both men were soaked with water from the icy stream in their effort to reach the safety of the Bund.

Realizing that their prisoners were dangerously chilled, Tom and George wordlessly sprung into action. They ushered them to the warmth of the living room hearth, and provided the prisoners with towels and blankets. As compassionate as Tom and George felt for the prisoners and their plight, the brothers-in-law realized that their escapees needed to be reported. While Tom stood guard George ran through the blustery wind to the Schuster's house to call Camp Upton to report their visitors.

v

My father, Thomas Clarke, was born in New York City in 1904 to Irish immigrants. He married my mother, Edith Hendrickson, in 1929 and they had three children. He worked himself to the top in the trucking business, managing many large trucking companies. When America got involved in World War II he enlisted in the army and was commissioned in the transportation corps. I remember him telling my brothers and me that he helped move the war from Africa through Italy to get home to us. He retired in 1945 and had achieved the rank of major. After the war he and his brother established a bonded messenger service. He retired in 1970 and died in 1980.

Marilyn Coffey was born in Brooklyn and married her childhood sweetheart, Hal Coffey, in 1954. They have three children. Marilyn has always been interested in politics and town government and served the Town of Esopus in many capacities culminating in being elected as the first woman supervisor of the town in 1982. She co-founded the Ulster County Supervisors Association.

In 1988 Marilyn accepted a position with the New York DEC as a Citizen Participation Specialist, joined the Ulster County Board of Elections in 1993, and retired after 25 years of government service in 1999. Marilyn is spending her retirement years being nanny to six grandchildren and quilting, gardening, and sharing quiet time with her husband Hal and many good friends.

Thomas Clarke 1929

COLD IN KOREA

Captain John Decker

I served in South Korea in 1954-5 just after the war, and after the prisoners had been returned over the "Freedom Bridge". But it was an uneasy peace. At any minute, we were told, another invasion from the North might come.

I completed officer's training in college and joined the Marine Corps in 1950. I got my commission after I graduated and was called up in 1954. We passed through Japan on the way to Korea. A funny thing-- we had to travel by Japanese sleeping train to another city in the South. My friend was 6 feet 4 and weighed 224 pounds, and I was a little over 6 feet and weighed 210 pounds. They put us in a sleeper that was 5 feet 10 inches in length, and we had to bend our knees to sleep. They had a little basin for washing. If one of us was out of the bunk, the other had to stay in bed as there wasn't room for two people to stand. It was kind of weird.

We went to a hotel when we got two days' leave. We saw all the shoes outside each room and thought it was a chance to get our shoes shined. The next morning we took our shoes in from the corridor-- still dirty. We called down to ask, "How come?" They laughed. "No shine shoes," they said. They explained that it was just not customary to bring your shoes into your room. We were in Nara, which was once the capital. Japan was gorgeous, with temples and such. It was a few years after World War II and there had been a lot of restoration.

All I can say is that Korea was a place that God forgot. There was just absolutely nothing there- a barren valley, weeds and dirt. We were there to make sure that we would be the police force, so to speak, if the North Koreans invaded again. We were near Freedom Bridge, three miles from North Korea. I was in command of a rifle company that was situated on a hill overlooking Freedom Bridge and Samachan Valley. Samachan Valley was loaded with land mines planted by US and South Korean forces, but the locations were not known. We never went in there. We were in the area replacing troops that had fought in the war.

We had some Red Alerts that indicated they were going to invade again, and everyone packed up and got ready each time. The threat of war was always in the back of our minds, but we were involved in training and other daily activities so we fell into our tents at night dead tired. We had rifles, mortars, machine guns, flamethrowers and bazookas that we had to keep in readiness. We had a rifle range, a demolition range, and other ranges.

I sent some of my members up into the caves overlooking the Freedom Bridge and the Samachan Valley to alert us if enemy forces were coming. Yes, it was lonely and tense up there but I knew that Korean prostitutes had been climbing up to keep the men company, as I could smell the kimchi the women were accustomed to eating. (kimchi is a pickled vegetable stew, made mostly with Korean cabbage and red pepper. It has a distinctive odor which I don't like.) I never caught them, though.

We went through the same kind of weather that "The Chosin Few" went through, which was severe winters and severe hot, humid summers. ("The Chosin Few" was Tenth Army Corps that was surrounded by enemy forces in the uplands of the coldest part of Korea. They lost many men.) We were dressed for the weather but the troops before us were not. We were in tents, wrapped up in sleeping bags. Rats crawled all over us in the night. You couldn't have a fire, and there were times the temperature would go down to zero to ten below. The only way you could keep warm was to toss pocket warmers into the bottom of the sleeping bag. It was a test to get up in the middle of the night to go to the outhouse. The outhouse was burned out every morning, followed by a mad dash there. Men wanted just to get warm.

We didn't have a whole lot of supplies. A sign was posted: "We've done so much for so little for so long that we can do almost anything with nothing."

A big problem was bathing. There were portable showers that wouldn't run on account of the cold. You got one shower a month if you were lucky. You know the old bowl your grandparents had? We had something like that as a washbasin.

It was just a terrible place to be. Just being there must have been terrible for the soldiers who fought before we came. They suffered with inadequate clothing and equipment. Before we went over we were sent to the California mountains to try to simulate Korea, but it didn't come close to what it was actually like being in Korea. It was terrible there.

John was born in Middletown, NY and graduated from Washington & Jefferson College. He worked for IBM for thirty-five years, served as Marbletown Town Justice for twenty-four years, and was a captain in the United States Marine Corps Reserve for seventeen years.

Interviewer: Lucille Weinstat

ASSISTING THE OCCUPATION

Annette Chait Finestone

When I graduated from the University of Wisconsin in 1941 it was in the depth of the depression and our involvement in the war seemed imminent. I had to find a job in a hurry so I moved in with my sister in New York City. I finally found a Christmas job selling jewelry at Macy's. With that experience I was able to get a steadier job at a smaller department store across the street from the Empire State Building. It paid $16 a week and I held onto it for a few weeks until my supervisor told me, "I'm going to have to reduce your salary."

On my next lunch break I went to the War Production Board in the Empire State Building and, even though my typing was nil, they hired me. A few weeks later that office was relocated so my sister and I moved to Washington DC. About the time of Pearl Harbor and our entry into the war I was transferred to the Office of Price Administration, where I eventually became an office manager in the personnel department. It was a fascinating job providing constant contact with interesting people. Our task was controlling prices and setting up rationing. Of course we were not liked by Congress, and the agency did not last long after President Roosevelt died. By this time the war had wound down in Europe, and then there was The Bomb and the war was over.

At that point there was a demand for civilian workers to go to Japan to assist the MacArthur occupation. Six months after VJ Day I was on board the *General Stewart*, a troop ship bound for Japan. My shipmates included six guys who had just graduated from the University of Michigan, where they had learned Japanese and become US Army lieutenants. Later they were my companions in Tokyo while we awaited our assignments. It was a hazardous two week voyage because of the numerous mines in the ocean. Our crew detonated two of them right in front of us. During the voyage I found *The New Yorker* article, "Hiroshima" by John Hersey, which was the first any of us had heard the real story of the horror and devastation caused by that nuclear device. It affected me deeply and I have often wondered, if I had read it before embarking would I have had the nerve to go?

On our arrival in Yokohama I was shocked. There were derelict ships littering the bay, and the buildings as far as we could see were in ruins. Our soldiers on board had not been indoctrinated in proper behavior, or disregarded it if they had been. They delighted in watching starving men dive into the bay to retrieve cigarettes, candy and anything else that they threw. The central business district of Yokohama had been spared, but the bus ride to Tokyo knocked all of our exuberance out of us. The same pattern of devastation met our eyes all the way, and the few people we saw were just pulling stuff out of the rubble. The center of Tokyo had also been spared, including the office building that was General MacArthur's headquarters, the building in which we were billeted, and– of course– the Emperor's Palace.

The office building in which we were billeted had been newly renovated. We were overloaded with Japanese women who had been employed as maids in an effort to help reduce the extreme poverty around us. The halls resounded with the sound "ononnay", which I assumed was someone's name. It turned out to be just a greeting. Without exception these women had long, black, luxuriant hair. But after a few days at our building they got bobs to look like us.

While awaiting our assignment my lieutenant friends were allowed to travel freely. With them as escorts I was able to see a lot of Tokyo. At one home we visited a table of food was laid out beautifully, but there was actually very little there. There was butter, but it was rancid. I was told I had better eat at least some of it out of respect, so I did. Another occasion was a party for American journalists, about two dozen people. After we had all imbibed too much sake, we were asked that each guest tell a story, sing a song or recite a poem. When my escort's turn came he got up and sang "Cino no Yoro" (Moon over China), a song that had been prohibited all through the war. A dead silence followed.

Whenever we went out we inspected the damage. Much of the city had been destroyed. We saw the flattened remains of the Mitsubishi aircraft plants. I'll never forget a group of lovely children gathered beside a ruin listening intently to a storyteller. He seemed to be an old man but it was hard to be sure since he was so emaciated. Hunger prevailed. The main rail station was a refuge for the homeless. Each day a few dead bodies were carried out of there.

After about six weeks I was assigned to the Fifth Air Force, based in Nagoya. While awaiting transport I was moved to the Army War College, which bordered the Emperor's Palace grounds. I could not enter but it was easy to see in. Amid all the destruction these grounds remained absolutely beautiful, a contrast that was almost unimaginable.

We went to Nagoya by train, a slow overnight trip in contrast to today's trip of a couple of hours by bullet train. My job was to place arriving American civilians in appropriate jobs. Here also an effort was made to employ Japanese civilians. Each of us American women was assigned a personal maid. I never figured out how to keep mine occupied. Whenever packages arrived from home with clothing or nonperishable foods we distributed them to our maids.

Female American civilians were not permitted to drive but I had no trouble finding escorts. On weekends we went out into the countryside. At first the people we passed in our jeep seemed afraid of us. I recall a woman working in a rice paddy that we passed several times, who finally stopped us and handed us some eggs. There were a few longer trips, including one to Toba Bay, the home of Mikimoto cultured pearls. The process had been invented by Mr. Mikimoto, who welcomed us in person. He allowed us each to select an oyster; if we found a pearl in it we could keep it. I was lucky to find a beautiful pearl which I later had set in a ring that I still prize. He was a bit of a clown and entertained us by doing cartwheels in his kimono. His whole operation seemed untouched by the war.

We visited a village that specialized in pottery and another that did beautiful cloisonné. For some reason the US Government permitted some crafts to be sold openly to Americans while others required special permission. Near the center of Nagoya was a large field in which citizens had brought huge amounts of metal objects to help in the war effort. We foraged among them and found some beautiful objects that I still possess.

Occasionally we saw returned Japanese soldiers march past with eyes averted. It now seemed hard to hate them. One day a friend and I were on a back road outside of Nagoya and it got dark quickly. We were lost. There was a small house and I knocked, as my uniformed friend would have scared the occupant. It was an old man who just could not understand my pronunciation of Nagoya. Finally he understood, repeated "Nayiowa", and motioned the direction. Then he gestured that we should wait, went into the house and came out with a small ceramic Buddha which he gave us. I still have it. It is old and beautiful. We found we had to be careful as the people were so kind and giving that if we admired something, they gave it to us.

I stayed in Nagoya until the following May when I felt my services were no longer needed and I was anxious to get home. I had been in Japan for fifteen months. I came home on another troop transport which docked in San Francisco, then boarded a train which seemed to take a couple of weeks to get to New York. I befriended two Japanese women. We left the train together at Grand Central, where there were several members of my extended family waiting to greet me. They hugged the Japanese women first, finally realizing that I was the one they were waiting for. I had to wait my turn. I wondered if those months in Japan had changed my appearance!

Max and Annette met in 1953 in New York, where they were working, and moved to Accord, NY, Annette's initial residence. There they took over operation of Chaits, Annette's parents' small hotel, and ran it for the next twenty-five years. Along the way they added two daughters. "The hotel was hard work," Max says, "but there were opportunities for fun too— especially for the kids." In 1978 Max and Annette sold the hotel and retired in Accord until they came to Woodland Pond in 2009. Annette's photos have been shown throughout the Mid-Hudson Valley.

Interviewed by Paul Lurie

Photos by Annette on the streets of postwar Japan

From a scrap metal yard

Sumo street competition

Woman with baby carriage

AN UNUSUAL ASSIGNMENT

Lee Gartrell

When I graduated from high school in Clay Center, Nebraska, I enlisted in the Navy. Since my father was a doctor, and I thought I wanted to be a doctor, I chose the Hospital Corps. My boot camp was at Great Lakes Naval Station. On VJ Day the war was over, and I was on my way from there for two months of training in San Diego to be a nurse. The training center was next to the lion enclosure of the San Diego Zoo, which provided a "jungle experience" to accompany my nurse's training.

When I arrived at the hospital I was assigned to a young man who had been burned over most of his body by a bomb blowing up in his battleship gun turret. He survived with severe burns over most of his body. He had developed keloids, scarring tissue that grows over the burns and looks rather grotesque. When his wife divorced him during this healing time he threatened suicide. My initial assignment was to be with him 14 hours a day, 7 days a week. I talked to him and to the man next to him who had had his jaw blown off in combat. The neighbor to my patient, although jawless, had a wonderful sense of humor which helped all around him enormously.

I was with my patient for six months, 14 hours a day, 7 days a week, with no break. One day a friend asked me, "Lee, what are you doing here still? This isn't right! You should talk to someone." I was 19 years old at the time. It hadn't occurred to me that perhaps I should have some time off.

A short time later I spoke to my supervisor at the hospital who sent me to Personnel, where I discovered that they had lost track of me. They didn't know I was there! They were shocked that I had been in such a difficult position for so long, and immediately moved me to the Eye, Ear, Nose and Throat ward, where I finished my term of duty. One of my tasks in this ward was to give back massages. One of the patients couldn't open up his fingers so couldn't use his hand. He asked if, instead of massaging his back, I could massage his hand and fingers. I agreed and did so for a number of weeks. When he left the hospital he was able to use that hand again. That was very gratifying to me.

I don't know whatever happened to the burned young man, but I think of him often. He made a whopping impact on my early experiences of World War ll.

Lee was born "90 miles from the geographic center of the US," in Clay Center, Nebraska. Lee enlisted in the US Navy Medical Corps and served for 18 months at Oak Knoll Hospital. He graduated from Nebraska Wesleyan University and Union Theological Seminary in New York. Ordained in 1954 as a Presbyterian minister, Lee served from 1957—1980 on the NYC Council of Churches in planning and research. He subsequently served 14 interim pastorates and, as the Executive Presbyter of Hudson River Presbytery, served as a problem solver for 93 congregations in the Hudson River Area. After retirement in 1994 he and his wife, Joyce, moved to New Paltz and he continued to fill vacant pulpits throughout the Hudson Valley. He and Joyce moved into Woodland Pond in January 2010.

MY VICARIOUS WAR

Richmond Greene

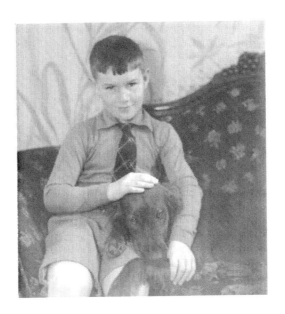

World War II ended when I was 15 so I never served in the Armed Forces. But I did get a taste of combat, thanks to a colleague of my father's. "Chick" was a Lt. Commander in the Navy and worked with Special Devices in Washington, DC. One Christmas when I was about 12 he invited me down to the Capitol, and among our adventures was a visit to Special Devices. Here they specialized in simulated training devices where you could learn to fly without having to leave the ground, practice bombing runs, etc., all without danger of losing lives.

So it was that I found myself in a tail gunner's bubble in a B-24 aiming at Messerschmitt aircraft with twin machine guns as they peeled off to attack. I shot at them and watched them go down. I remember that I registered a high score. Then I moved on to the cockpit of a Link Trainer where I was desperately searching the instrument panel trying to find out why my plane was fast losing altitude. The biggest adventure, however, was acting as bombardier in the nose of a B-24 bomber. As we glided over the sleeping city of San Francisco the Norden bombsight guided us over the target. A buzzer rang, I pushed a button, and watched as a string of bombs fell and exploded below. You could see where they landed and flashed in a line. It was hard to believe we were not actually in the air.

It was a vicarious war. No risk. No courage needed. But I did get a feel of it that I shall never forget.

Rob Greene grew up in West Hartford, CT. His parents were both school teachers. He attended Amherst College and Union Theological Seminary. For fifteen years he served as a Congregational minister in New England. Then he trained as a psychoanalyst at the C.G. Jung Institute in NYC. He now has a private practice in New Paltz and is also a professional artist.

WHEN WE WERE VERY YOUNG

Trina Greene

1943

A small flock of young children wearing red and white striped shirts and shorts with a stripe down the side run up a hill to its highest crest under a blue sky, stretching their hands upwards to snatch at frail paper shapes floating downward. They have been dropped from a silver plane droning high above and flurry downward in all directions. The children catching some of these pastel shapes note that they are small paper "bombs" with writing on them. The children do not read the propaganda print: the fun is in the trapping of these delicate sky borne shapes. These American children do not hear the whine and thunderous explosions of real bombs dropping on other real children in Europe.

I was nine years old when the war in Europe ended, seemingly too young to know anything about the desperate struggle of the past six years in war-torn countries across the Atlantic. We had a Victory Garden with furry-leafed tomato plants, red radishes, rows of lettuce, and brilliantly painted zinnias rooted firmly in our yellow clay soil. I loved to sit between the narrow rows of giant zinnias and look up from under their leaves at patches of sky. I was not thinking of the children in England or in Germany looking up at their skies from houses with shattered roofs, or from beneath piles of rubble.

I *was* told at every meal to finish the food on my plate, and remember 'the starving children in Europe'. And when we traveled on the trains between Philadelphia, New York and Connecticut, I used to smile a gap-toothed smile at the handsome young men in military dress packed into the aisles of the train. But beyond the occasional blackouts when dark cloth was put over our windows, and memories of my mother shifting gears at 35 miles per hour and turning in coupons for gallons of gasoline, the war was a soundless struggle, a territory of destruction out of focus, far away.

This formed one layer of my childhood consciousness of wartime. I did not realize that the photojournalism of *LIFE* magazine and the news films preceding the feature film at the cinema would form far more powerful substrata. Every Friday afternoon *LIFE* magazine would arrive with our mail and I would dive for it, devouring the photographs taken by war photographers. War photography was in black and white then, but the uniforms holding together the bodies of dead soldiers were unmistakably water or blood soaked, vividly captured by the camera, as were the expressions of young men in helmets braving bayonets and grenades, sometimes with tear-soaked dirt streaking their faces.

In front of me were spread out the smoking cities of Europe and children dressed in knee socks, sweaters, winter overcoats and sturdy school shoes (or barefoot) in winter, climbing over enormous piles of rubble. Many of these schoolchildren no longer had a school or a home to return to, or parents. This was the thought that brought a sense of abysmal loneliness and lost-ness to my heart: no "Mo-ther!" to wail to, no "Daa-dy!" to pick one up with strong protective arms.

There was a book I used to read titled something like *Young Heroes of the War*. Each chapter was about a child in a war-torn country such as Norway or France. There was the bravery of a child who flew down the Alpine snowfields with gold bricks adding to the weight of his sled, to aid the Allied troops. There was the story of the little girl who carried important messages to the Allied Command in the head of her doll. I was breathless when I read of these courageous children and wondered if I could ever be as brave, knowing that the Germans in their steel helmets and antiaircraft guns and monster tanks were nearby.

LIFE magazine depicted the death of Mussolini and the women dressed in widows' black, their faces twisted by bitterness, firing round after round into his body. As the cameras of the wartime reporters continued to click away and I leafed through *Life* magazine on my lap, the bodies of massacred Jews began to pile up before my eyes in concentration camps, and the starved faces of Europe's Jews peered at me through barbed wire. I was there in the crowds of German youth who stiffly saluted Hitler. I spied on Goebbels and Himmler as they rode in open vehicles through the streets of Berlin or Paris.

I was only nine years old when the war ended. Sitting in my bed with chickenpox and again turning the pages of *LIFE* magazine, I looked at the Nazi criminals wearing earphones at the Nuremberg Trials. I examined their expressions closely: would the atrocities they had performed show on their faces? With their shaved heads they looked vulnerable and ordinary. Then I turned the page and saw them standing in front of the gallows that would take their lives. When I turned the page again, however, there was a row of photographs depicting each of these men after being hanged: a row of heads at odd angles, eyes closed. Despair and revulsion swept through me and, sitting there in my pajamas, I wept. I had come face to face with obscenity – both in the manner of killing and in the act of coldly photographing the result. I did not know that my young spirit could know such despair.

I dreamed through my childhood of German generals walking overhead, their boots sounding sharply on the attic floor above. As an adult, I still have a recurring dream that I am in a concentration camp and we are about to be marched to some terrible end. I am trying desperately to collect the right clothes and boots for surviving such a long march.

In many ways I feel that the photographic journalism of the '40s was far more powerful in the way it affected my understanding of the truly rotten fruits of war than the short films on television today. It was more detailed; it was created under life-threatening circumstances. In order to get clear shots the photographer had to be in the thick of the fray. As the camera examined the faces of war perpetrators and war victims it was able to capture something of the human spirit – its luminous and dark sides. The journalism of that time marked my young spirit as surely as if I had been there. We need a new and current language to convey the horrors of war, a new way of communicating this to the very young, other than through fuzzy television bites. As a senior all I have to do to connect with World War II is remember what I discovered at the age of nine.

Trina Twyeffort Greene was born in Philadelphia and grew up on the Main Line. After graduating from Vassar she earned a diploma in Painting from the Boston Museum School and a Masters Pi Lambda Theta in Teaching from Harvard. Although trained as a painter, she was drawn to sculpture and has spent the past thirty five years in that field, as well as teaching Sculpture and Hand Building in her studio. Her work is informed by folk art, early Classical Greek Sculpture and myth, sculpture of the Renaissance and, currently, by an indigenous American sense of spirituality-

being part of the earth and those forces which create and maintain it. She just finished a commission to be cast in bronze, a life-sized sculpture of the 11 yr old slave, Isabella, who grew up to become Sojourner Truth, the famous spokesman for women's rights and racial ethics. She is married to Rob Greene, a Jungian psychoanalyst with whom she shares a love of art and symbolism, and is the stepmother of four children, and grandmother to four more.

EXPERIENCES ON THE HOME FRONT

Elizabeth (Betsy) Haight

I grew up in East Hartford, CT—the home of Pratt and Whitney Aircraft and Hamilton Standard Propeller. These plants were strategic in the production of aircraft engines, and therefore our town was considered a possible target for attack in case enemy planes reached our shores.

During the 1940s I was in elementary school. The war was declared over when I entered high school in 1946. In those early years we had air raid drills at all times of the day and night. If we were in school, we had to leave the class and go into the hallway, sitting down with our backs against the wall and our arms covering our heads. I do not remember it as a scary time, perhaps because we knew it was a practice.

When the air raid drills came in the evening, all houses and public buildings had to participate in "blackout". This meant all windows and glass areas had to be covered with shades or blinds of some kind. My father and mother decided to cover the windows in their large bedroom, along with the adjoining bathroom. My dad built large wooden "covers" for the windows which were light enough for Mom and us kids to put up. The reason my mom had to do the job was because Dad was an air raid warden for the streets in our neighborhood, and he had to leave for duty with his flashlight and hard hat as soon as the warning siren sounded.

Like most patriotic Americans, my father and mother found ways to help the war effort. My dad, as a father of three, was not eligible for the draft. He did become eligible later and went for his physical for the Navy just a week or so before Germany surrendered. Therefore, he never did serve in the military. He did, however, work as a personnel director on the second shift at Hamilton Standard Propeller. As for many people, this factory work for the war effort was done along with a regular day job. Under these circumstances it was difficult to have much family time. We were fortunate we could ride in the car with Dad on the weekends, as he took care of his insurance and real estate business before reporting to his second job at the war plant.

Mom was actively involved as a Red Cross volunteer instructor. Classes were held in various parts of the town to inform and instruct people in the proper methods of caring for the injured in case of an enemy attack. Another one of Mom's important jobs was keeping our ration books straight. A family received books for each member in each category. Books for shoes, butter, gasoline, meat and probably some others that I have forgotten. The books contained coupons and were issued monthly.

I believe this is when margarine was introduced as a substitute for butter. It was my job to mix the little yellow capsule into the soft, white vegetable oil mixture so that it resembled butter. I remember sitting on the kitchen stool and squeezing and squeezing the plastic bag until the color was as uniform as I could get it. Then Mom would open the bag, squeeze the ingredients out into a dish—and voila! We had butter!

It seems that everyone had a "victory garden". No matter what size yard, there were gardens at every home. We were fortunate to have a good size lot as part of our property, so Dad and Grandfather planted a large garden. My grandfather was a talented and dedicated farmer at heart so our yield of vegetables was plentiful. This was considered an important part of the war effort.

As I read over what I have written here, I am sure my story is very similar to what many others have as memories. Perhaps mine is a little different as I lived a short distance from two major war manufacturing plants.

I grew up in East Hartford, CT, the oldest of three children. My father was a concert violinist and gave violin lessons in our home, so music has been an integral part of my life. I graduated from Hood College in Frederick, Maryland with a degree in early childhood education. While at college I met Craig Haight, who was a student at John Hopkins University. Craig and I married in August, 1954, and I enjoyed many years as a Methodist minister's wife.

When our four children were all in school I taught pre-school in Ridgefield, CT and New Paltz. I retired in 1989 after fourteen years as the receptionist for the VanDeWater and VanDeWater law firm in Poughkeepsie. Craig and I moved to Woodland Pond in October, 2009, where I enjoy singing with the Pondaliers and the many activities offered here.

FROM REJECTION BY THE NAZIS TO RECONSTRUCTION

William Helmrich

I was born on March 4, 1925 in Cologne, Germany. Our early years in Cologne were normal and civilized. My parents had three sons and I was the middle one. They had a small clothing store business and were successful in every way until 1933 when Hitler told the Germans that they could not do business with Jews. My dad was forced to close his store and had to find another way of making a living. It was then that he started exploring the possibility of leaving Germany and coming to America. But how?

My dad had a cousin, Rose, who was married to Sam Wachtell, a well known attorney in New York City, where they lived. They agreed to meet my dad in Paris in 1935, where my dad discussed our wishes. The Wachtells were receptive to becoming our sponsor. Some of our relatives in Germany were quite negative. They told my parents that they had no knowledge of English, no special skills, three children, and no wealth. They would have a hard time in America. Besides, the economy was bad. The trouble in Germany was soon to blow over. My parents ignored all that well-meant advice. During 1935 and 1936 they settled their business, sold what they could, and obtained clearances from the German government. We were called to Stuttgart by the American government for medical and other examinations, and in 1937 we got our visas, passports and tickets. We gave up Cologne, went to Le Havre, France, and sailed on the *Ile de France*. We arrived in New York on Oct. 26, 1937. We were in America!

This was well before Kristallnacht, knowledge of concentration camps, displaced person camps, and the mass murder of six million people, mostly Jews. This was before annexation ("Anschluss") of Austria and Sudetenland, the invasion of Poland at Danzig and Pearl Harbor. The invasion at Danzig was the beginning of World War II. We lived in the Bronx and my father became a peddler of household goods in Yorkville in Manhattan. After building a clientele he was able to make a living.

At this time the United States had no draft, a small army, and a small navy. In September of 1939 World War II started and things changed. I was 14 years old and graduated high school in January of 1941 at age 16. At that time I enrolled in City College of New York as a freshman in mechanical engineering. In January, 1944 I was drafted into the U.S. Army and sent to Fort Dix in New Jersey. I was processed to join the Combat Engineering Battalion in Camp Carson, Colorado. There I did basic training and during the week of June 6, 1944 (D-Day week) we had completed basic training and were transferred to Fort Jackson, South Carolina. We arrived within a day or two of D-Day wearing woolen uniforms in South Carolina. (It must have been better than Omaha Beach.)

We continued training; in October,1944 we were sent to England, then in December of that year to France and on to Luxemburg. The name of our outfit was the 1255th Combat Engineering Battalion. The Battle of the Bulge had begun and was in full force. Our assignment was to recapture the city of Vianden in Luxemburg, which the Battalion did on February 11-13, 1945. These three days were our main participation in combat and we had numerous casualties in our unit.

After that we moved to Aachen, Germany, then towards Bonn in April. Roosevelt died and Truman became president. The Germans thought they would win the war, but on May 8, 1945 the war ended and peace was declared.

Those who survived did well after the Battle of the Bulge. The atomic bombs shortly thereafter made further combat unlikely. Most of us had two or more years of service and qualified for discharge after VE and VJ Days, and many qualified for college in some of the best schools in Europe. My discharge was a year later; I decided to come back to the US.

About that time I asked for a transfer to military government and I got it within a few days. (I had a Military Occupation Specialty, qualifying me as an interpreter of German.) After several assignments I was assigned to a detachment in Krumbach, Germany. (Bavaria) It was the equivalent of a county, with a population of about 20,000 people. Our task was to open public schools, re-establish civil government (mayor, police department), open the courts, staff the jails, etc. We had about 12-15 GIs, wonderful officers, and the support of other US government functions.

We accomplished our mission and I came home in spring of 1946. My war was over.

Bill was discharged as Staff Sergeant in April, 1946. (Editor's note: Commanding Captain Carl Whitney: *"The Special Branch is charged with handling a vitally important phase of the de-Nazification Program…Sergeant Helmrich has performed his duties as supervisor in a superior manner, exhibiting a wide knowledge of the subject matter, of the German people under investigation, and has carried out difficult assignments with unusual thoroughness and devotion to duty."*

Bill received a bachelor's degree in mechanical engineering from CCNY in 1947, a master's degree in mechanical engineering from NYU in 1950, and his New York State professional engineering license in 1952. He and Edna were married in 1950. Bill began work at IBM in Kingston in 1955 and retired in 1988. They have a son and daughter and three grandchildren. Bill and Edna moved to Woodland Pond in 2011.

Editor's note: Bill's sponsors, Rose and Sam Wachtell, must have been extraordinary people. Here are words spoken at the unveiling of the monument for Sam on Sept. 10, 1944:

It is the wish of Rose Wachtell that I speak to you here today. As is understandable in a long life, I have often stood at the graves of people who had touched my heart. However, as yet, I had never spoken at a grave site where the word "death" left me helpless, speechless and overpowered by feelings—leaving me broken, stammering and sobbing.

And so this morning, I decided to write down what I might say to you. At least, the calming achieved by writing words down will permit me to speak to you in a controlled, quiet manner. This surely would be Sam's wish.

Hundreds and hundreds were saved by Sam Wachtell, year in, year out. He did not wait to be called—in kindness he would meet all suffering, so as to alleviate it. And so it might happen, that in a hundred years a son will ask his father, "Dad, how is it that we were able to be saved by coming to this country?" The father then must reply, "My son, at that time there was a man by the name of Sam Wachtell—he saved us. I did not know him because he died young but your grandfather often told me about him. He never failed to say that he was the _finest_ man that he had ever met." A noble and pure human being, that's what he was, and that made him outstanding. He was a quiet person, yet an exemplary one as he went through life. He was a witness who believed that purity (honesty) was indeed possible. Above everything, he set a good example, because in a re-birth of human souls he can then be an influence for improvement.

I said earlier that until today I had not spoken at a grave. Today I am still not talking at a grave. This monument is only a symbol that spans a life between birth on earth and death on earth, a life that has found fulfillment through earthly activities, and has ended. And so, Sam Wachtell's first life has ended, but his second richer life, that of _example_ that he gave to all, that has already begun. When we leave here and again step out into life, we should know the following: We did not come to a funeral ceremony to mourn; we have come to a celebration of thanks. Thanks that there was a Sam Wachtell, that there was, and still is, and that he will be there in the future!

Richard Beer-Hofmann, translated by Bill Helmrich

TWO WARS

Lawrence Hiller

As a 10 year old living in Montreal, Canada, I had no experience of war when World War II broke out in 1939, but I had heard some stories. One was that my Uncle Ed was gassed during World War I, and that my dad met my mother in England and she became an English war bride. One of the most vivid stories I recall is that of a Christmas Day during World War

I when the Allies and enemy troops stopped shooting at each other for a few hours and climbed out of the trenches to extend Christmas greetings.

My experience of war began in 1939 when a young neighbor came running down the street yelling "Warsaw is in flames." I didn't understand. I thought it was some kind of machine until later discussions revealed that Hitler was bombing Poland. World War II had begun. The next day my 16 year old brother, Jim, went to the recruiting station to inquire about service. He didn't return home that night, and the next day my mother learned that he had enlisted and was on his way to England. My 18 year old brother, Gerald, followed soon after. Jim served in North Africa and Italy before being shot in the leg by a German sniper. His injuries ended his service and he returned home. Gerald was in a hotel in London when a V2 rocket hit, causing a head injury which led to a lifetime of seizures.

Many times I went to the Windsor train station in Montreal to see the wounded soldiers returning to a heroes' welcome. I was attending school and in the summers I worked on farms in Alberta while farmers' sons were fighting the war. It was hard work but a valuable experience. By 1945 I was in the Sea Cadets, preparing to enter the Navy, when the war ended. The outpouring of sheer joy, and the celebrations in the streets of Montreal will be forever in my memory.

During the 1950s in Quebec there was a large radical group of French Canadian residents who wanted to separate the province from the rest of Canada. The separatist movement caused much harm and unrest; government property was destroyed and laws were passed that made it difficult for English speaking people to stay and work in Quebec. As my family was English speaking, we and other non-French families left their homes and jobs to start over in other provinces across Canada. This was indeed a sad time in Canadian history.

I moved to Esopus, New York in 1951 where my fiancée, Anne, joined me a year later. We were married two weeks after her arrival. On our wedding day I received a draft notice by mail to appear in Albany for a physical. The letter began with "Greetings," and Anne exclaimed, "What a wonderful country, they send you greetings on your wedding day!" Our honeymoon was cut short.

The Korean War was on and I was drafted into the U.S. Army, where I served in Fort Carson, Colorado. This period was hardest on my new bride. Only 19, she was left to adjust to a new country and a small town. Fortunately she made friends easily and started a new job. While in the army I received my US citizenship. After my two years of service I returned to Esopus and secured a job at IBM, where I worked for 38 years. Anne and I raised two children and celebrated our 60th wedding anniversary on August 30, 2012.

Edited by Halema Hassan

MY FOUR UNCLES

John F. Ineson

1942

I was just a little kid in 1940 and there was a lot of talk about war in our home and the neighborhood and on our Stewart Warner radio. I didn't know a lot about war but I did know a veteran of World War I and what I knew scared me. About twice a week this man, the veteran, would come home from work drunk and severely beat his wife and their two sons, one of whom was my best friend. His family excused his behavior because he had been injured and gassed in the war. Obviously I was scared of veterans and, as the war came closer to us and members of my family began preparing for war, I was worried what would happen to them and what they would be like when they came home. This story is about my four uncles, their war experiences and the impact on our family.

Uncle One

My mother's oldest brother was what we would describe as a dashing, handsome man. He was slight of build, had a neatly trimmed mustache, drove a four door Lincoln convertible, was a highly successful dentist, had achieved the highest award the Boy Scouts could give and was a real ladies' man who loved to party. In retrospect we would see the conflicts of his life.

When it became apparent to my uncle that we would eventually be drawn in the war he became impatient and decided to join the Royal Canadian Air Force (RCAF) where he hoped to become a fighter pilot and fight the Nazis in Spain. This was an impulse decision and his family barely had a chance to say goodbye. I have one picture of him after he came home on leave in his RCAF uniform and he continued to look dashing. Then something unforeseen happened. For reasons I was not told (remember, I was a little kid) he was washed out of the RCAF and came home. He did not live to see the end of the war.

Uncle Two

My father's older brother had a Ph.D. in forestry and worked for a department in the government that worried about trees. He had married a woman who was an evangelical Christian. Whenever they visited he would sit quietly, while his wife terrified my sister and me by quoting the Bible and insisting that we pray with her.

Sometime during the war he was transferred to the War Department (I did not know why they needed a tree expert). Immediately after the Japanese surrender he was assigned to General MacArthur's staff and he and his wife and two daughters moved to Tokyo. His job was to help the Japanese restore the country's forests which had all been cut down for fuel since Japan had had no access to oil or coal. It was a very important job and he reported directly to MacArthur. Rather than live on a U. S. Army base they chose to live in a Japanese neighborhood, which must have been a real challenge at the time.

Not long after settling into their home in Tokyo they began to get to know their Japanese neighbors and to understand the extreme hardships being endured by them as an aftermath of the war. Eventually my uncle and aunt decided that rebuilding the forests was not enough and that it was more important to bring Christianity to the Japanese.

My uncle resigned from his government position and they joined a missionary organization. At first they worked in Tokyo and then moved to Okinawa where they assisted in establishing a very powerful radio station for transmitting their evangelical message to people all across the Asian-Pacific area. Eventually they moved to the mountains of Haiti where my uncle used his talents to build a large hospital and where my aunt could use her training as a nurse. They were in Haiti for many years until their retirement in Florida. After their retirement they occasionally visited us. My aunt would now terrify our kids while my uncle would either sit quietly in the corner or go off and play golf.

Uncle Three

My mother's other brother was a trained electronics engineer and in the late 1920s worked for Western Electric. His specialty became sound motion picture systems and he was responsible for installing these systems throughout the Near East. We had pictures of him riding a camel near the Sphinx and sailing on the Nile as well as cards he would send as he flew in a Ford Tri Motor plane between Arab countries. He installed equipment in the private theaters of Saudi princes. Eventually he left Western Electric for a more prosaic but ultimately more profitable life. He built the second drive-in movie theater in the country and was in the process of starting up several others when World War II arrived.

Not long after Pearl Harbor the Navy contacted my uncle and made him an offer he did not want to refuse. He was directly commissioned a Lieutenant Commander and sent to Florida to what was then Banana River Naval Air Station (now part of the Kennedy Space Center). His assignment was to provide hands on training to the crews of Navy PBY aircraft in the use of a new invention, airborne radar systems, which the crews were to use to locate Japanese ships in the Pacific. Although the work was arduous and often dangerous he managed to meet and marry an internist/diagnostician MD working at the Navy hospital. After the war they returned to Connecticut, had a daughter, built several profitable theaters and he became the beloved uncle of our extended family.

After he died, he was dressed in his uniform and given a full military funeral.

Uncle Four

My father's younger brother graduated from college just before the outbreak of the war. He had been trained as a classics scholar and artist and was probably headed toward a career in academia. The draft got him almost immediately; he went into the Army where he was trained as a tank mechanic. He arrived in France soon after D-Day and was involved in the fight to liberate France.

His unit discovered that he could speak French so he was initially sent out into the countryside to scrounge up anything that would make the life of his unit more comfortable. He was so successful that soon he was sent ahead of the troops to arrange for Resistance forces to protect bridges and other similar structures.

Not too much later he was transferred to the Office of Strategic Services (OSS) and eventually to its successor, the Central Intelligence Agency (CIA) where it was discovered that this tank mechanic was natively fluent in several European languages. We never really knew what he did thereafter, although once a picture of him appeared in the newspapers. He was dressed as a United States Air Force officer and was questioning a Russian who had defected with his plane. He also became fluent in several Slavic languages and Greek.

He married an Austrian woman and by the time he came home for a visit he had spoken so little English in the past years that he could not remember the names of common household items. He came home one more time for about a year after he had been "burned" and it was too hot for him in Europe, but he did go back until it came time to retire.

When he did retire he and my Austrian aunt came home on an ocean liner and I met them as they came ashore. I had not seen him in many years and expected someone from a John LeCarré book. Instead, out from the ship terminal came an aging, overweight man, wearing a loud checked sport jacket, a too small hat and carrying a big old cat.

They retired to Cape Cod where he did some beautiful wood carvings and oil paintings. He was responsible for getting me interested in carving. Not long before he died he was able to tell me some more about his life.

John was born in Cleveland OH in 1933 and lived there until 1946 when his father was transferred back to Hartford, CT. John graduated from Wesleyan University in 1955 and received an MBA from Cornell in 1957. He met his future wife, Lori, at Cornell. They were married in 1958 and have two children. Their move to Woodland Pond was their thirteenth and hopefully last move.

Childhood illnesses gave John the chance to become an early and avid reader and by the time he was seven he was regularly reading Book of the Month Club selections. As he outgrew his ailments he became an avid Boy Scout and also delivered (and read) the Cleveland Press.

John spent his entire career in the computer industry and thinks back on it as a continuous adventure "where every day when you woke up the things that were impossible yesterday are doable today." He remains involved with computers and the Internet.

A MOST UNUSUAL IMMIGRATION

Lori Ineson

Lori and her grandmother

Leaving family friends and the country of one's birth are wrenching decisions that thousands of immigrants to the United States have made and will continue to make in the future. In the late 1920's both my mom and dad made their decision to leave Germany and their families behind and immigrate to the United States. The reasons were many, but foremost in my parent's case was the desire of their parents to get their children out of Germany before war broke out again. The rumble of war was clearly being heard. Both my mother, living in Pirmasens near the French border, and my father from Munich were urged to join siblings who had already immigrated to the New York area. My father, a master builder and cabinet maker, packed his tools, a few clothes, and a German-English dictionary. Max was ready for his big adventure.

My mother Olga's immigration transition was most unusual in that it eventually involved the FBI and President Dwight D. Eisenhower ("Ike"). Olga, the youngest in the family of five children, spoke German, English and French fluently and was eager to see her brother in Brooklyn. Traditionally, children left home from eldest to youngest in age. My mom, the youngest in the family, was devastated when her older sister Elsa received her passport and visa. At the last minute Elsa had a change of heart. She absolutely refused to leave her parents. My mom jumped at this unexpected opportunity and convinced her parents that she could pass for Elsa in her passport photo, which was somewhat fuzzy. So my mom, Olga, arrived in the United States as Elsa Schaaf in 1928 and, upon entry, resumed using her real name, "Olga".

Mom's brother had arranged a job for her as a governess whose primary duty was to teach the children French. In time she met and made friends with a lively Viennese woman whose husband's younger brother, Maximillian, had moved in with them. Would Olga like to come for dinner on her day off? Olga Schaaf and Max Grassl were married on Sept. 27, 1930.

I was born a few years later after the newlyweds had saved some money to build a house for their family. The house was not quite completed in the late1930's when my grandmother in Pirmasens decided she would travel to see her latest grandchild. This time Elsa decided to go along for the visit. We were living in small quarters but grandmother played with and spoiled her latest grandchild, and was pleased with her new son-in-law and the house he was building for his wife and child. Grandmother stayed for several months. She had hoped to see the house finished and furnished with the lovely dowry she had brought along but felt it was time to go home. Elsa decided that she liked living in the US and would stay a while longer. Unfortunately "a while longer" lasted beyond the date the US and Germany declared war.

Living in our house now were two sisters each with the same name on her visa. As far as the Immigration Department knew there was only one visa, one Elsa Schaaf. Olga Grassl, who chose to use her given name instead of Elsa once she was in the country, was now married to a husband with American citizenship papers and a daughter born in the USA, a bona fide American citizen. Who and where, if there was one, was the second Elsa Schaaf? Or Olga Grassl?

It was a scary time and it wasn't long before the FBI arrived to try and solve the riddle. Aunt Elsa was out for a walk and did not return home until after the FBI left. The two FBI men made a cursory check of my parent's papers, including Dad's citizenship papers and my birth certificate. They checked the closets, cabinets, and desks. They took along with them all of Dad's cameras, his console short wave radio, and all photo albums and photographs. We were told they would be returned after the war. We never saw them again.

The FBI informed my parents, in front of a rather frightened young child, that if we did not behave as Americans they would have the right to place me, the born in the USA American, in a "good American home." I guess it was a good thing they didn't know I spoke German as well as English. It took a long time to forget those words, and the idea of being taken from my family made me mute in front of strangers.

At that time there was a saying that you could tell a FBI car by the sound it made coming down the street. It's true and scary. Aunt Elsa and I would disappear out the back door when the FBI was heard rumbling down the road. As the war progressed the visits decreased but never completely stopped until peace was declared.

Eventually neighbors realized what was going on, and those good folks let us know that their doors were always open for unannounced visits. My best friend was a Jewish girl who lived next door. Jill's mother would call us in from the yard when the car rumbled by, and we would have a cooking lesson to take our minds off the big black car. My mother would reciprocate when it was safe, and let us cut out cookies when she went on one of her baking binges.

My mother, whose house in Germany was bombed during World War I, started a campaign to make our family self-sufficient. She stocked up on canned goods, medicine and other essentials. She didn't go so far as sewing old coins in the hems of our coats in case we had to make a fast get-away, as her mother had done for her family in World War I. Then again we didn't have any gold coins.

We were sure of a supply of milk (unpasteurized) from the farmer down the road so thank goodness we didn't need a cow. But, according to my mom, chickens were a necessity. I had a bantam chicken, Goldie, which was exempted from necessity status and had free roam of the property. Dad built a lovely chicken coop which was stocked with laying hens, a rooster and some baby chicks. The coop had a large fenced enclosure outside for a daily whiff of air, and once or twice a week they were permitted to roam free. Strangely enough, they didn't venture far away. My job was to collect the eggs.

For a while Mom thought we would be OK with chickens and a vegetable garden. Then one day she announced we would need two pigs, just in case something happened to the chickens and they didn't last the duration of the war. The pig sty that Dad built was not quite as lovely as the chicken coop but required, according to my mom who had never lived near a farm in her life, a wallow with water in it for the two piglets to keep cool in the summer, and also for them to keep themselves clean and be happy as they grew. The wallow didn't work as planned so Mom went to Plan 2. Every weekend she slung a rope around the necks of the pigs, now named Emil and Antoine, and led them one by one unto the backyard lawn where she scrubbed them with a bristle brush dipped in Ivory Flakes. After they were hosed off they were the pinkest happiest pigs, rolling around on their backs on the manicured lawn. After the war, because none of the family could bear to eat them, we left the premises while a professional slaughterer did his job and the meat went to a charitable organization.

Mom had ambivalent feelings about supporting the war effort for either side. If she helped the war effort, would she be helping kill her relatives in Germany? If she didn't, would the US lose the war and, in turn, would we become prisoners of a foreign country? She somewhat resolved her split desire to help both sides by contributing only to war drives that would help keep people alive, i.e. it was OK to gather milkweed for vests. (Saving lives was good.) Mom and I were near the top of "number of bags of Milkweed pods picked" whenever there was a drive. Same for food and clothing. War stamps, however, were bad because they bought arms and ammunition which killed people.

Dad made sure I bought stamps for my war bonds at school. He slipped me money on the sly. Mom, never catching on and feeling guilty, started knitting socks like crazy, sending packages of socks and wonderful cookies she baked to the husbands and sons of friends and neighbors preferably serving in the Pacific. You gotta love my mom.

As the war progressed the FBI became less visible, neighbors remained neighbors and friends remained friends. People appalled at "those Germans living down the road" still had kids who would climb the trees outside our property shouting, "Nazis live here" and worse from time to time.

As the war ended people were looking to buy, build or fix up existing homes and, in adjacent areas, large estates needed attention too. Dad was back in business big time. On a memorable visit to a longtime and wealthy client Dad was asked to build a small, old-fashioned colonial style cottage on the estate. It would have a room large enough to hold a good sized rug that at one time lay in front of George Washington's desk, with enough room for the desk too. The cottage was also to have a modern bathroom and small kitchen, but the living room, bedroom and den had to look as if they were built in colonial times. Dad loved the idea and agreed to build it. He did have a question though. "Why the bedroom?"

he couldn't resist asking, "Is Washington coming back to sleep in it?" He client replied "no" and smiled as he told Dad that he would be building the cottage as a weekend hide-away for Dwight D. Eisenhower; it was a big secret and he was to tell no one.

Dad told him he had a secret, too. He explained my mom's illegal status. Did he think Ike might have some helpful advice? The client said he would ask Ike to set aside some time for a short visit the next time he came to look at his new hide-away home.

The client threw a huge Christmas party every year. Everyone who worked there, visited there, or was remotely connected with the estate was invited. The past Christmas President Eisenhower had been there and we had spoken with him. I remembered him as a very charming, genial person, so it was comfortable sitting on the patio with Ike the next spring. Dad explained what our problem was. Ike was reassuring, told my mom he was sending a bill through Congress in a week or two and he would ask to have a rider added, addressing her problem.

The president was good to his word. Mom received a US visa a short time later. She was told to go to Canada, stay as long as she liked and, on her return, make sure her visa got stamped on the Canadian side of the border by Canadian border guards. When she reentered the US she was legally in the country for the first time. As quickly as she could she took her citizenship exam and pledged her allegiance to the United States! Thanks IKE!

I am an only child, born to immigrant parents, hardworking people, who established a family in a foreign country with loving care and devotion to both family and country. My dad was a talented builder who designed and built the house we lived in. He worked for others, many of whom were less skilled than he, until he and my mom had saved enough money to buy land and build their own home. They chose to build on a wooded lot outside of White Plains between Purchase, NY and Quarry Heights, northeast of White Plains. I have never figured out why the postal address always was and still is White Plains, NY!

I grew up bilingually and attended a 2 room, 2 teacher elementary school about a mile away from home. Best teachers I ever had! Jr high and high school were in White Plains. We had a big yellow bus that took us to these schools in the morning and returned us home late in the afternoon. The fact that each classroom had more kids than the entire school I came from required a lot of adjustment. As foreigners often do, my parents expected excellence in academics and my grades were expected to put me on the college track. My dream school was Cornell University, although I had never seen it or knew anyone who had attended. In my senior year at Cornell I met my future husband. We introduced our parents to each other the day we graduated and announced we were getting married. There was dead silence for about ten seconds and then both sets of parents, in unison, said, "Wait a year." So we did. Two children, four grandchildren and 14 related moves later we will be celebrating our 55th anniversary. Woodland Pond is the end of the road, but not the end of the journey.

ESCAPE FROM BEIRUT

Dorothy Kerr Jessup

Kerr family passport photo, 1941

Mackie and I were excited. It was May 20th, 1941, a month before school would be over, and the day we started out for America the long way around the world. The short way, through the Mediterranean, had become too dangerous after the Nazis defeated France, and especially after Italy joined the war on the Nazi side. We knew about the mines and enemy submarines and that it wasn't safe for passenger ships because our older sister, Marion, had left for America the previous summer on the last one to go that way.

We had come home from school for lunch only a few days earlier to find our parents hurriedly packing our entire household, putting some things in crates to store, and even selling a lot of things, all without any prior explanation. They simply told us only we'd be leaving soon for America, because the Germans had taken over the Aleppo airport in northern Syria. We knew that was dangerous, and we knew about the war in Europe. But neither seemed especially scary to us, because in our childish minds, Aleppo, Europe and even the submarines in the Mediterranean seemed far away.

We were living in Beirut, in the province of Lebanon, then part of Syria, at that time a French "mandate." Our father was a professor at the American University of Beirut (AUB). We lived in a spacious two family house, overlooking the Mediterranean on the AUB campus, where we had the freedom to safely roam and play with little adult supervision, as Lebanon and especially that campus, were at that time considered very safe. We children attended a small community school just outside the campus. There were four of us, but Mackie and I were closest in age: he was nine and I was eleven that year. Our older sister Marion was by then in college in America, and our little brother Dougy was only four - too young to understand even as much as we did about the war.

Mackie and I were well aware of the war in Europe, especially the Nazi invasion of Holland, Belgium and France. Since we were living in a French territory, the fate of France seemed relevant, even to us children. We knew that most of France was by then under German control, and we knew that the Vichy French (who still governed southern France and Lebanon) were not the same as the Free French, who were still fighting on the Allied side. We knew that Italy had joined the war after the fall of France, and we even knew there were enemy submarines and mines in the Mediterranean – the reason we had to travel the long way around the world.

We learned most of what we knew about the war from our father. Our parents listened faithfully to the BBC, and discussed the war at mealtimes. Dad had posted a large map of Europe on our dining room wall, and every day since the war began in September 1939, he marked various troop positions with colored pins. Everything shut down for two hours for the midday meal in Mediterranean countries in those days.   People started work early and returned to work through late afternoon, but the middle of the day was family time, for dinner together followed by a nap. Our father was a teacher by nature (as well as by profession) and dinner was an ideal time for him to explain to us what was happening in the war – the war in Europe, that is. We didn't hear much about the battles in North Africa in 1940, and certainly not how badly the war had been going for the Allies after the fall of France.

Mother was a teacher too, but it was Dad who told the war stories, and stories of their adventures in Turkey, where our parents had met helping the Armenians at the end of World War I. Dad had gone there with the Near East Relief, and Mother as a missionary teacher before they went to Lebanon. I never realized until I read my father's memoirs after he died, how dangerous that experience had been, based on the horrible things they'd seen happening to Armenians in that region.   All we knew as children were exciting stories about how Dad had helped Armenians escape from Turkey, and Mother and Dad's orphanage for Armenian boys who'd lost their parents.   They didn't tell us the horrible, dangerous, scary parts about what happened to those boys' parents. And they didn't tell us the horrible, scary things they undoubtedly knew were happening in Germany and elsewhere under German occupation.

We knew about the Nazi concentration camps, because after France fell, all German citizens living in French colonies (including Lebanon) were ordered to return to Germany. Those who refused were to be "interned." Dad had several German colleagues at AUB, and we knew their families, though we'd never known they were Jewish or what that meant : only that they chose to be "interned" in Lebanon rather than going back to Germany and probably a concentration camp, which was definitely something to be avoided. When we left for America, the two German families we knew best joined our American exodus.

Our father treated the war as an opportunity to learn, and our trip as an exciting adventure. We were to travel almost around the world. And right now, we were headed for Palestine, on our way to Egypt, where we would find sea transportation from Suez, down the Red Sea to the Indian Ocean and eventually around the world, via the Pacific, to America. It was a beautiful, clear day and all five of us were crowded into a taxi traveling south down the main shore road along the Mediterranean coast. Our excitement wore off as our prolonged taxi ride went on and on, down the Mediterranean coast through Haifa, then east to Jerusalem. By today's standards, that may not seem an especially long trip, but in an antiquated 1930s model automobile, traveling on narrow roads through many towns and villages, it took close to eight hours. We arrived in mid-afternoon in Ramallah, where we were housed at "Harb's Casino" along with a number of other American families we knew from Beirut. (It was actually a family friendly pension, but the Arab family who ran it probably didn't quite catch the not so subtle difference, and neither did we. Neither did it occur to us to wonder who made all these arrangements in advance, on such short notice. Harb's Casino was located inside a lovely walled garden, with trees to climb and plenty of place to play. And we liked Ramallah. In those days, it was a simple Arab village in the country, where donkeys, camels and barefoot children still wandered in dirt roads, along with women clothed in traditional Arab dress carrying large earthen jars of water on their heads.

We spent the next several weeks visiting the holy sites, including Dome of the Rock, the Wailing Wall and Bethlehem, floating in the Dead Sea, and playing quietly in Ramallah. Dad bought me a little notebook to use as a diary, so I could keep a record of our experiences as we traveled. I made daily, detailed entries during our stay in Ramallah, though little about the war. On June 8th, 1941, however, I noted: "The English are now fighting in Syria" and on June 18th I wrote:

> "This afternoon, Daddy told us some stories. He told us how Sidon was captured. It was pretty queer. Three Australians were...(*separated from their company*) when they were just outside Sidon. They walked into the (*Vichy French*) headquarters and the sentry wasn't sure more

weren't coming so they surrendered to them. Then they went inside and the officers thought the same as the sentry, so they surrendered also. When the *(Allied)* army actually did come they found the officers had already surrendered."

The invading Allied army consisted of English, Australian, and Free French forces. According to news reports at the time, many of the "Vichy" French troops sympathies lay more with the Allies than their own Vichy high command, so such stories of easy surrender are credible.

We stayed on in Ramallah for several more weeks. I remember wondering why we stayed so long in Palestine when we were supposed to be in Egypt, waiting for passage via Suez and the Red Sea to Australia. Dad told me we were waiting for a visa, and that satisfied me. On June 22nd, I noted in my diary :

"The English have captured Damascus now, but Germany has attacked Russia and probably will win."

Actually, we were in more danger from enemy forces closer to us, though we children had no idea of that at the time. While things were going relatively well for the Allies engaged in Syria, they'd been hard pressed to defend their bases elsewhere. The British positions in Iraq and Egypt had been especially precarious, following their devastating losses in Greece and Crete which left them poorly equipped and far outnumbered by a very well equipped German army. As a story in *Time Magazine* [0] put it

"These men were in no shape to undertake another heroic defense. They and all the British forces in Egypt were woefully thin on heavy equipment. Of all the armored strength available before the Greek campaign, reportedly just one brigade remained in service in Egypt."

But when Hitler launched his surprise invasion of the Soviet Union on June 22nd , diverting substantial German air and ground forces to the Russian front, the situation reversed long enough for the British to regain control of the Egyptian border. That questionable move on the Nazi's part allowed the Allies a period of respite, allowing them to re-build their forces and replenish supplies. And it allowed enough time for refugees like us to travel through Egypt with relative safety.

Our parents, who diligently followed the news, must have known about the precarious Allied position in Iraq and Egypt during June '41, as these events were reported in their main news sources: *Time Magazine* and the BBC. Under the circumstances, one might expect them to have shown some signs of worry or nervousness, but none of the grown-ups we knew seemed especially worried, so we hardly noticed the one adult who was: Dr. Hampel, one of Dad's much younger colleagues, was said to be having a nervous breakdown under the stress of keeping his young family and pregnant wife safe during the trip back to America. Since all the other grown-ups (even the Oppenheimers and Myers's, who were German and Jewish) seemed unperturbed compared to Dr. Hampel, it didn't occur to us that there might be good reasons for concern.

Our parents kept the worrisome bits of information to themselves, while we children innocently played in the safe walled garden of Harb's Casino. Dad was finally able to get us a visa for Egypt, and we were all set to leave when Mackie got sick. Dougy and I each had a bout of whatever it was for a few days, but Malcolm took longer to recover, so we couldn't go to Cairo with the rest of our American group. In my diary, I wrote on June 26th: "Malcolm is much worse today, so we can't go tomorrow." Then finally, on July 6th:

> "Yesterday we went to Lydda by car. The train was late in coming to the station, but we got on all right. We got *Wagon Lits* (compartment with sleeping bunks) as far as Kantara. The rest of the way (which was during the night) we rode by day car. It was crowded with soldiers. They all stood up so we could sit down. There were two very nice ones. I stood out in the aisle so I could look out the window. They told me about all the things we passed.

Most of the way was sandy desert that blew in the face. In some places there were forests of palm trees...

On the way (to Cairo) from Kantara, there were some Italian prison camps. They were very bright because of course the Italians would not bomb their own prisoners. The two soldiers who were talking to us said that they were R.A.F. They said that every morning they lay under their aeroplanes and worked on them.

They asked me what I wanted to be when I grew up. I said that I wanted to be a nurse. They said 'Don't be a war nurse, It's not nice and you have to be brave.' They asked Malcolm what he wanted to be but he didn't know. One said, 'Well, don't be an airman. It's no good.' "

In Cairo, we were housed at the American Friends Girls' College, along with the other Americans we knew from Beirut. The school had been closed for the summer, as Cairo was unbelievably hot in July. In those days, with no air conditioning, electric fans, or refrigeration in our quarters, our main relief from the heat was taking long cold baths.

While waiting for news of a ship to take us to Australia, we visited the pyramids and the Cairo zoo, but spent most of our days indoors, because of the outdoor heat. In the evenings, we'd play outside in the school's walled yard. On the other side of the wall, though we could not see them, we could hear Australian soldiers singing at night : they sang Christmas carols. We children, discussing this among ourselves, decided that the hot Egyptian July evenings must have reminded them of Christmas in Australia, where Christmas is in mid-summer. I remember thinking they must have been homesick. We had no idea how young these soldiers must have been, or how exhausted, following the intense battles they had fought in Libya, Greece, Crete or on the Egyptian border, and certainly no idea of the extensive casualties they must have witnessed among their comrades.

Sandbags were stacked up against buildings everywhere, as protection against flying shrapnel in case of air raids, and we did experience occasional air raids. On July 12th, I wrote in my diary : "Suez was bombed last night." Later, I wrote:

> "One very interesting thing that happened while we were in Cairo, were the air raids. There were two... The (college's) shelter is said to be the 2nd best in Cairo. There were fans and mattresses down there, and so you could go to sleep. Some people said they had seen shells bursting."

While we were in Cairo, all three of us got sick again for a few days, but then Mackie became more seriously ill and had to be hospitalized for quite a while.

On July 27th we learned that there was a ship leaving for Australia that would have room for our American group, but we couldn't go with them because Mackie was still in the hospital. Mother and Dad conferred with his doctor, and were advised to wait for a ship with a doctor on board. Every day after that, Dad went to the Embassy to find out when a ship with a doctor might be leaving. About a week later, he came back with the news that on the following day there would be a ship likely to have a doctor on board, but we'd have to go to Suez, packed and ready to leave, to find out for sure. Our parents convinced Mackie's doctor to discharge him, and Dad brought him back to our rooms from the hospital.

That night, we were packed, ready to go, and almost ready for bed when the air raid sirens sounded. Mother said we had to go to the shelter. Dad refused, and said he wouldn't move Mackie just to go to the shelter. Mother insisted. Dad said the planes wouldn't be bombing Cairo, but only flying over on their way to Suez. Dougy and I wanted to stay with Dad and Mackie to watch the planes, but Mother kept insisting, and she won. Well, partly: Dougy and I had to go to the shelter with her, while Dad and Mackie stayed upstairs in our rooms and later told us what fun they'd had watching the planes and searchlights from the bedroom window. They didn't see any bombs, so it seems Dad was right.

We had to leave early the next morning to cross the desert to Suez before it got too hot. We left in a taxi at seven a.m., reaching Suez by mid-morning. The driver pulled up to a spot where we could see the entire harbor, and we just sat in the car and looked with horror at a mess of half sunken ships. Some were still floating, but abnormally tilted; others were almost completely submerged. Not a ship there was still upright. It looked as if those Italians flying over Cairo the preceding night had hit their targets very well, after all. Dad told us not to worry until we had the full story. He told the driver to pull up to a low, warehouse-type building and went inside. We waited in the car with Mother and the driver, waited and waited. It was getting hotter. Finally, Dad emerged from the building smiling, and holding some papers. Mackie and I shouted all our questions at once, "What happened ? Why did it take so long?" Dad kidded around a bit. He said it had taken a long time because the men inside wouldn't believe he was the man on his passport, because when he signed the papers they gave him, he'd forgotten how to spell his middle name (a family joke, because the name was long and awkward: Elphinstone.) Then he told us that when he'd shown the men the papers from the Embassy, they'd replied that the ship in question had a doctor on board, and appropriate hospital facilities, but it didn't take passengers. It was a troop ship and had *never* taken passengers, and certainly not American passengers. We never found out how he managed to convince them to let us go on board anyway, but somehow he did.

Mackie and I were still a bit dubious, because there was no seaworthy ship in sight. Again, Dad told us not to worry, because it was anchored well outside the harbor. He paid the taxi driver, and we all got into a motor launch with our luggage. The motorboat went through the harbor, passing all the sunken ships, and further, but we still couldn't see anything. Dad kept telling us not to worry. After a while, we saw a small grey spot off in the distance - tiny , at first, but gradually seeming larger and larger. Then finally, after riding in the motor launch for well over an hour, we pulled alongside the most enormous ship we'd ever seen in our lives: a huge grey passenger ship that had been converted to a troop transport before being finished, the then largest ship in the world: the *Queen Elizabeth*. We looked straight up at it from the motor launch and couldn't believe anything could be so enormous. We had never even seen a building that large, let alone a floating ship. Because the ship was anchored way out at sea, there was no dock or gangplank to make boarding easy, so we had to climb up some long, rather precarious stairs from a floating raft tied to the ship. But Mackie and I were game to climb anything there was to climb, and he, though just out of the hospital, was already showing miraculous signs of recovery, so we scampered right up the side of that enormous ship.

Things didn't go quite so easily when we reached the top of the stairs. We were greeted with surprise by a couple of ship's officers. Dad had to spend another eternity convincing one of him that our being there wasn't a huge mistake. The officer told him this wasn't a passenger ship. Dad showed him the papers he'd been given from the Embassy in Cairo, and more with appropriate stamps of approval from the officials in that shed in Suez. I have no idea how he managed to convince him, but Dad had a knack for appealing to reason, and the officer at least took the time to listen.

Through all this, we children were on our very best behavior. We didn't need to be reminded, because we wanted to stay on that marvelous ship so badly, we were terrified this ship's officer would say "No." Mackie and I just stood there, as still as could be, beside Mother. Dougy may have been more responsive to the friendly Australian officers who smiled at us as they squeezed by. Some may have said something, or tousled his blond head, and he would have smiled back in his characteristic, outgoing way, because that's how Dougy was on that trip. He charmed all those men: the Australian officers, the ship's crew, and possibly even that particular ship's officer, because the officer finally decided to let us stay on board.

He gave us two adjoining cabins on the promenade deck. These would have been first class accommodations in peacetime, but in keeping with the ships' status as a troop carrier, each cabin had extra built-in wooden bunks. That suited us fine, because we three kids could share one cabin with Mother and Dad right next door. Though our cabin was small, it had a real window opening out to the promenade deck and the sea, allowing us welcome sea breezes once the ship got moving. (Even first class cabins weren't air-conditioned in those days, and the *Queen Elizabeth* had not been built to sail in tropical waters.)

We were told that the ship wouldn't sail for a few more days, until fully loaded with troops on leave, supplies and German prisoners. We knew about the prisoners, because they took their daily exercise on the promenade deck, passing our cabin window in long, heavily guarded lines. We knew there were nurses on board, though we rarely saw them. But it didn't occur to us there must also have been many wounded soldiers lying down below in the ship's hospital we never saw: young Australian survivors of those intense battles where the Allies suffered such heavy casualties in the Mediterranean region. No one mentioned them, so it didn't even occur to us to wonder why there was a well staffed hospital on board.

We ate with the Australian officers, in their nice air conditioned dining room. That first evening, after supper, Dad suggested we go out on deck. It was cooler once the sun went down, and quieter, without all the bustling daytime activity. There was not much to see, as we were far out from the harbor and there were no other boats around. Mackie wondered where the cruisers and destroyers for the convoy were, so Dad asked one of the crew standing not far from us. The guy explained the *Queen Elizabeth* never traveled in a convoy, because she was so much faster than any other ship a convoy would only slow her down. Then he offered to show us around. There were several decks besides the promenade deck, all with life boats of course, but what impressed us most were two huge cannons the crew had named "Belching Bertha" and "Bertha's Baby," located at the bow and stern. Around noon every day, the crew fired off each cannon, just to be sure they worked properly in the event they were needed.

While we were exploring the deck, we noticed the ship had started moving. That seemed odd, as we'd been told we'd be anchored outside Suez a few more days for loading. But she had clearly turned south, and was moving along at a pretty fast clip.

We stood right over the bow, looking down at the waves and porpoises playing alongside. Dad asked more questions, and we learned this was to be a regular routine: every evening, at dusk, the *Queen Elizabeth* pulled anchor and sailed south down the Red Sea till about 3:00 or 4:00 a.m. Then she'd turn around to sail north again, reaching an area some distance south of Suez in time to drop anchor before sunrise to resume loading. This was how the British kept her whereabouts a mystery from enemy planes on their nightly air raids. Of course the ship was blacked out at night, so when we went to bed each night, we had to choose between keeping our room dark or leaving our window open. Since it was so much cooler sleeping on the moving ship than in our hot rooms in Cairo, we happily lay there in the dark.

A few days later, the *Queen Elizabeth* pulled anchor for the last time and cruised on out to the Indian Ocean. By that time, we'd established our routine. Except for mealtimes, when we went with Mother and Dad to the air conditioned officers' dining room, and the afternoon movies we regularly attended with Dad and the ship's crew, we spent our days exploring on our own. It didn't take us long to acquaint ourselves with the ship's facilities and crew. One of the first things we found was an elevator operated by a British sailor who'd lost an arm. Dougy must have asked him about it, maybe even on the first day, because they quickly became great friends. (Dougy, in his four-year-old way, would have simply asked: "Why do you only have one arm?" and the guy, instantly disarmed, would have explained he'd lost it in the war.) Dougy mentioned several times during that voyage that he'd like to be a one armed elevator operator when he grew up.

Our other special friend was the ship's Librarian, Billy, a middle aged retired sailor from London, who in very few words, conveyed to us his pride in the British spirit in responding to the hardships of the war and the nightly air raids. But most of the time, Billy told us funny stories, teased us, and if we got a little too noisy and wild, threatened to tickle us, which immediately produced appropriate results.

The crew generally looked out for us – none of them seemed to mind our running around the decks and hallways, or asking them questions. Naturally, we were sufficiently in awe of those men to be on our best behavior. Meanwhile, Dad liked to hang out in the air-conditioned Officers' Lounge, chatting with Australian army officers over coffee or beer. We'd drop in to visit him from time to time, but stay only long enough to cool off. Mother usually stayed in the cabins doing chores, or sitting in a shady spot somewhere on the promenade deck, reading or talking with the army nurses.

Dad picked up a lot of information about the war and ship in the Officers' Lounge. One of the men he enjoyed talking to was a British news correspondent, Reggie Glenn, who had spent time in North Africa and later interviewed some of the German prisoners and their guards on board. Dad told us some of what he'd learned: It seems many of the German airmen refused to believe they were traveling on the *Queen Elizabeth*, as they'd been told they'd succeeded in sinking it a year during a raid on Liverpool. We also learned that one of the airmen, who'd participated in a devastating air raid on Coventry, England, couldn't resist bragging about it; one of the soldiers guarding him, from Coventry himself, had lost his home and family during that air raid, and was so enraged he stabbed the Nazi airman with a bayonet. Fortunately for both, the airman was only wounded, so the stabbing had no dire consequences. According to Reggie most German prisoners were more compliant, though some were convinced their U-boats in the Indian Ocean would attack the *Queen Elizabeth* and rescue them.

Mackie and I were a little worried about the submarines, despite the reassuring canons' daily boom. But Dad explained that by not traveling in a convoy, the "Lizzie" (as the crew called her) was able to fool the subs by following a zig zag route across the Indian Ocean. That, coupled with her speed, made it difficult for any U-boat to track us. So though traveling through dangerous waters on a battle grey troopship, we felt secure and safe, and continued happily exploring the "Lizzie, " until one day something unexpected happened that *really* frightened us.

We'd taken a new route on our daily rounds and discovered a flight of stairs we hadn't noticed before. There was a closed door at the bottom, so we scampered down to see where it went. I turned the knob, the door opened and suddenly, we realized we were in an entirely new part of the ship, one we hadn't seen or even heard about. We stepped into a strange new hallway, and straight across was an enormous room filled with crude wooden bunks, three or four tiers high. In or around the bunks were well over a hundred women and children. We were stunned. Who were all these people? Suddenly, a military guard appeared out of nowhere. He was not the kind, friendly type we'd come to know in our earlier explorations. This man spoke harshly: "Who are *you* ??" We froze. I don't remember when we started crying, but I do remember trying to explain we'd come from "upstairs" and that we were American passengers.

He didn't believe me, and warned us not to try fooling him. He warned us there had never been either Americans or passengers on this ship, so there was no point in pretending. Then he grabbed all three of us, roughly, by the arms, dragged us into the giant room, and ordered us to show him our mother. He marched us down an aisle between the rows of bunks, saying "Which one is your mother? Show me where she is." By this time, all the women and children in that crowded room were staring at us, and we were all three crying. He kept on, harshly: "Where is your mother?" and between sobs, Mackie or I would stammer "Upstairs." Somehow, we knew those women and children were German internees. It was clear they were prisoners of some kind. Perhaps we heard them speaking German, which we would have recognized, though we didn't actually speak the language. Mostly, I remember being absolutely terrified. We couldn't understand why that stern officer wouldn't believe we didn't belong with those apparent prisoners, because we were speaking to him in plain English, without a foreign accent. We had known enough English-speaking foreigners in Beirut to recognize differences in their accents, but it never occurred to us that our own accent may have sounded foreign in those days to an Australian or Englishman.

We never knew the details, but word must have got out among the ship's crew that there were some children among the German internees claiming to be Americans and refusing to identify their mother, because finally, one of the crew came in the room and said politely to the stern officer, "Sir, I've heard there *are* some American children on board." So the officer told someone else to check on that, and eventually another sailor came and escorted us back upstairs. By this time, Mother and Dad had already started looking for us, concerned that we hadn't turned up as usual when the canons fired at noon. But I don't recall any scolding. We must have been so obviously upset by our misadventure, they hadn't felt that necessary.

The *Queen Elizabeth* arrived in the Fremantle harbor (western Australia) in mid-August, where she stayed a few days to re-fuel and replenish food supplies. She remained some distance out from the shore, as there were no docks in that port large enough to accommodate a ship her size. But by this time, we were far enough away from the war zone that there was no need for a nightly cruise outside the harbor to evade enemy bombers. Some Australian troops disembarked at Freemantle, but otherwise, those on board were not allowed on shore. While we were there, the *Aquitania* (carrying our Beirut friends) came into the harbor, escorted by a large convoy. The *Aquitania* had left Suez more than a week ahead of us, but though she sailed a more direct course than the "Lizzie's" zig zag route, arrived at Fremantle a day later. We learned later from our friends that they'd been so worried about German U-boats tracking them they'd slept every night in their life jackets, and had boat drills every day.

Though both ships were anchored reasonably near one another, we weren't allowed to communicate between ships except by naval signal. Dad managed to send a cryptic message to one of his colleagues aboard the *Aquitania*, letting him know we were on the *Queen Elizabeth* and would probably be arriving in Sydney around the same time. We watched the ships flashing signals to one another by Morse code.

We arrived in Sydney about a week later, around August 22nd . It was winter in Australia, so Mother took us right away to buy appropriate winter clothing. We re-united with our American friends from the *Aquitania* and spent the next few weeks at a windy beach resort south of Sydney that would normally have been closed for the winter months. The American consulate had apparently arranged once more for a place to accommodate our entire group.

Except for the fact that many Australians were serving with the Allied forces, Australia seemed far removed from the war zone in September 1941. (That would change within only a few months.) I remember being impressed by the brightly lit streets in Sydney each night, especially the colorful neon signs. Still, there was evidence of the war everywhere: soldiers in the streets, battle reports in the newspapers and in movie theaters. Even as children, we sensed an undercurrent of fierce loyalty among Australians towards England and the British Empire. One felt it especially in the movie theatres, before the newsreels came on, as the audience rose proudly together to sing "God Save the King" with a contagious energy that filled those enormous rooms.

We stayed in Australia through mid-September, when we were able to book passage on an American liner, the *Monterey*, this time as ordinary cabin-class passengers. Despite the frequent boat drills, we encountered few signs of the war during our trip on the *Monterey*. The ship was painted bright white, and brightly lit at night. There were no canons being fired, no prisoners marching on the decks, and certainly no internees in bunkrooms down below. We were able to disembark freely at every port we entered (except Samoa, where there had been an outbreak of some contagious disease). We took a beautiful bus tour in New Zealand, where we spent a couple of days in late September (their early spring.) We visited grass huts and laughed at policemen wearing short white skirts in the Fiji Islands. In the port at Honolulu, lovely Hawaiians greeted us with flowers and leis. We took another beautiful bus tour in Hawaii, where we picnicked at Waikiki Beach. Except for some huge rolls of barbed wire covering various beach areas at Waikiki, we witnessed no sign of the impending war in the Pacific. I remember asking Dad about the barbed wire, and he thought it was probably there to deter a possible enemy attack by sea. But that was the only sign anyone was even thinking about the war since we left Australia.

The Hampels - Dad's anxious younger colleague and his wife - were with our group on the *Monterey*, and Mrs. Hampel's baby was born the day we crossed the International Date Line, meaning he had two birthdays. We kids thought that was wonderful, and so apparently did an L.A. newspaper, since it published a nice little story with a photo of Mrs. Hampel with her 11 day old son following our arrival in Los Angeles on October 6th. But poor Dr. Hampel was still in no shape to escort his young family back to the American east coast, so Dad flew to New York with the Hampels the following day, to be sure they reached their east coast relatives safely.

Meanwhile, we traveled across the country with Mother by train, to Philadelphia and then New Jersey, where we spent another month with our grandparents (Dad's parents) and Aunt Marion, Dad's sister, who lived in neighboring towns. In November, we moved to Newark, Delaware, so Dad could spend his sabbatical year working with a professional colleague at the University of Delaware.

On Sunday, December 7th , the announcement came over the radio that Pearl Harbor had been attacked. We had invited friends from Beirut for dinner that day, so Dad moved the radio to the dining room, and we all huddled around it to listen while we ate. Soon after that we saw the photos of Pearl Harbor in the newspapers and newsreels, and beautiful

Hawaii now looked like Suez. It struck us especially, since we'd just been there. We remembered the rolls of barbed wire on Waikiki Beach and guessed that it wasn't the attack that came as a surprise, but that it had come by air, rather than by sea.

It wasn't long before there were signs of the war everywhere. Aside from the newspapers, every time we went to a movie (which was quite often, because we didn't have television in those days) there would be newsreels of the war. Suddenly, all Americans were paying attention, and the Pacific was another war theater. The following summer,   Dad had to go back to his job in Beirut (again, the long way via the Pacific) so we moved back to New Jersey, closer to relatives. We spent the following year in Ventnor, on the Atlantic coast, where we had to observe nightly black-outs, and then moved for two more years to Princeton, where the town was filled with young naval officer candidates being trained at the university.

In those various places, we experienced the rest of the war mainly as other Americans did, with rationing, shortages, and a father far from home.   But there were some differences: In a period of four years, Mackie and I attended six schools, and had already seen more of the world than most other American children we knew. Though scarcely well off by American standards, we knew how lucky we were to have been Americans during World War II.

Though the country we'd left had been only briefly under Nazi occupation, that had been an unknown when we had departed Lebanon, and could well have ended quite differently. Given the potential danger, we were lucky to have been entitled simply by birth to (American parents) to the unquestionable right to return to America in a time of danger. We'd been lucky not to have had to worry (except for a scary half hour) about being "interned" as enemy aliens. We'd been exceptionally lucky to have been allowed to travel in comfort and fully protected through dangerous waters, while refugees elsewhere were crowded onto ships in cramped quarters. We'd been lucky to have reached the American mainland before the U.S. entered the war, and above all, we knew how lucky we'd been not to have suffered more severe hardship and pain. Those of us here in the U.S. had a relatively easy time of it, for the real war was far away.

Dorothy finished high school at Northfield School in MA and returned to Lebanon for a year before going on to Wellesley College, where she met her future husband, Phil, a student at Harvard Law School. They raised three children in NYC, where Dorothy also got her PhD in sociology at Columbia University. Later she became professor of sociology at SUNY, New Paltz, where she taught for 26 years.

Mackie grew up to be a political scientist, Near-East specialist, and professor at UCLA. He then became president of the American University of Beirut where his father had previously taught. Mackie was tragically assassinated on campus by the Islamic Jihad (Hizbollah) in 1984.

Dougy gave up the idea of becoming a one-armed elevator operator after elevators became automated and, instead, followed in his father's footsteps to become a professor at Western Reserve Medical School in Cleveland.

Dorothy on donkey

Dougy and wallaby, Koala Park, Australia

Sakkara pyramids, Egypt

Dorothy on camel, Ramallah

Consul Palmer with Kerrs

Swimming in the Dead Sea

Wallaby picnic

PLANE CRASH

Donald "Pete" Johnston

Photo taken by a member of the crew

I was at the navigator's desk in the Plexiglas nose of the B-17 bomber when I saw the first sign of trouble for our raid on Nazi Germany. One of the two engines on the port side of the four-engine plane suddenly exploded and burst into flames. There was no immediate explanation for what was soon classified as a "mechanical failure". The consequence was made known to the crew right away by Jim, the pilot, a first lieutenant who was the aircraft's commander by virtue of his job. "We've lost an engine on our left side," he shouted calmly into the intercom, "and we must abort the mission. We're returning to base immediately."

The date was December 3, 1944 and the fighting in World War II was winding down in Europe. Our B-17 was en route in early-morning darkness to join other Flying Fortresses attached to the U.S. 15th Air Force based at Foggia, Italy. The rendezvous was set for 20 minutes of flying time out of Foggia. All of the planes would then head for Germany to bomb a large terminal containing military fuel oil. Raids like this one had become a daily ritual designed to punish the Nazis' capacity to fight back. The targets were primarily military bases and airfields, munitions factories and storage depots of fuel for airplanes, tanks and other military equipment.

Earlier in the war, Italy was an ally of Germany but surrendered when U.S. and Allied troops invaded after winning bitter battles in North Africa. The United States subsequently strengthened its holdings in Italy to increase its pressure on Germany. Not surprisingly, the targets were strongly defended by Nazi anti-aircraft weapons. I can recall flak ripping through the fuselage below me continuing up through the navigator's desk and skimming past my face as I leaned down to study maps on the desk. There was no way of predicting where the flak would come and nowhere to hide from it. We had to rely on luck and the difficulty of the Nazi gunners hitting speeding targets at high altitudes.

A "hit" of our B-17 by the anti-aircraft specialists would be catastrophic for our crew because our plane was loaded to capacity with explosives for the scheduled raid. The bomb bay was full of bombs; the gas tanks held 2,700 gallons of gas for the long trip to southern Germany; the oxygen system was primed to keep the crewmen alive and alert at altitudes of around 30,000 feet, and the strings of .50 caliber bullets laid on the floor adjacent to the six machine guns manned by trained gunners in the fuselage and the navigator and the bombardier in the nose.

The machine gun was just one of the navigator's responsibilities; the other two, of higher priority, were charting courses to targets for the pilots, and recording notes on everything that happened on a mission, including the intelligence briefings before and after a mission.

To make the situation more uncertain for me, I wasn't flying with my own crew or in my own plane; I was on loan to another crew whose regular navigator was grounded because of illness, and there were no substitutes on standby. For a couple of weeks I alternated flight days between my own crew and a navigator-less crew. On the current mission I didn't know any of the crewmen except for the pilot with whom I conferred about the mission prior to take-off. Also, I was surprised to learn that the co-pilot for this mission was not the regular first lieutenant but a lieutenant colonel assigned to conduct a periodic performance appraisal of the plane and crew.

The unexpected loss of one-fourth of our power stirred concerns in my mind that the day ahead could be the most threatening of my life. The burning engine itself was not necessarily a killer, but a mechanical failure could lead to a crash and fatalities. We got the crash, but fortunately not the fatalities. That last mission was my 43rd. If I had flown seven more and achieved 50, I would have made my assigned quota and been rotated back to the States.

Not long after the first engine explosion, on our way back to our base, there was a loud "Bang!!" on the right side of the aircraft. A second engine had exploded and caught fire, and with our power now reduced to 50 percent, the plane started to lose altitude. Jim the pilot quickly seized the intercom: "We have to make an emergency landing," he told the crew, speaking rapidly. "We're still in friendly territory, and over sparsely populated farm land. There seems to be adequate empty space for a landing and no encroaching buildings. But get out fast and run for cover. We may have a huge explosion, or the whole plane may catch fire."

Remarkably, I was the only guy who was hurt seriously; all the others escaped with only minor or no injuries. I was at my usual navigator's place in the nose and busily recording everything that was happening. The only access to the rest of the aircraft and exits was up a narrow crawl space behind the pilots, whose many instruments were above the nose. To my distress, when I reached the crawl space the plane was sinking downward into the emergency landing and I was fighting to go the opposite way— against gravity. Push as mightily as I could, I couldn't move past the narrowest part of the space. I was trapped, a prisoner of gravity. I couldn't get out of the nose!!

Meanwhile, as the sun was just coming up, the pilot descended and circled for a landing in a pasture. Dazed, I watched through the Plexiglas as the plane dropped quickly ever closer to the ground. Scary, as I stared at the earth coming closer and closer to me. "Why is my whole life not passing through my mind?" I wondered, recalling an old familiar saying. That's the last thought I remember having on the plane. We crashed and the aircraft plowed through the turf for at least a thousand feet. The Plexiglas was torn apart, and I was tossed through to a resting place about three feet in front of where one of the engines stopped skidding. Close call.

The next thing I remember is a crewman shaking me into consciousness on the ground and picking me up quickly to rush me to the ditch where the other crewmen had taken refuge. "Come on!" he admonished me, "the plane may explode." Jim was true to his word and landed the plane without casualties -- except for me (and that was not his fault).

Incredibly, there wasn't any explosion or any large fire; just a small fire that worked its way back slowly through the fuselage. The crewmen were huddled in a large ditch in the cold pre-dawn weather. "Are we all here?" one of them asked, I learned later. Another counted and replied, "Only nine."

It was risky to return to the burning hulk, laden with explosives. But two of the crewmen volunteered to search for the missing man. They hurried back to the aircraft and quickly found me lying face down and unconscious, a yard in front of an engine where the emergency landing stopped. By the time the rescuers carried me to the ditch, I had regained consciousness and was screaming for them to take it easy on my left leg. "It's killing me!" Because the knee wasn't working, the leg hung loose and limp as the rescuers moved as fast as they could to beat any expected explosion from the burning plane. For whatever reason, an explosion never came and we hustled safely to join the rest of the crew. I learned later that two of the four ligaments that hold together and control the knee joint--the anterior cruciate and the collateral --were completely ruptured and useless as is.

The rescuers were temporarily tired from their rescue efforts, and wanted to shift my body to other crewmembers crouched in the ditch, waiting for transportation back to their base and an ambulance for me. Purely by coincidence, the closest guy for taking and holding me happened to be the fill-in lieutenant colonel. That unplanned gesture by such a high-ranking officer drew a few coughs and smiles from the enlisted men. But the colonel refused to change. He knew that movement caused severe pain in my leg, and he held his ground. Because we were in the boondocks with no buildings nearby, we had to sit in the bitter cold for more than an hour before transportation arrived, including an ambulance.

The ambulance took me to the small hospital in Foggia, but there was no surgeon there prepared to repair the damage. I was immediately rushed to a larger hospital in Naples, but there was no knee specialist there. So after a do-nothing week in Naples, I was put on a packed hospital ship for a 30-day voyage through Nazi attack boats to the United States. We landed in New Jersey and I was deposited in Tilton General Hospital at Fort Dix for treatment that eventually lasted a year--for a knee operation and recovery.

In 1945 knee replacements were quite new and rare, so the chief orthopedic surgeon chose another possible solution. He tried to construct a hinge for the knee with body material taken from another part of my body. After a year of healing, physical therapy and exercise, the doctors in

1947 reluctantly pronounced the operation unsuccessful. The knee was still wobbly and painful. The doctors and hospital administrators wanted to give me a medical discharge but I said, "No, I want and deserve a second opinion." So they transferred me to Halloran General Hospital on Staten Island. My hopes rose, but after another year of treatment and special exercises, my knee was still a handicap.

During this period, though, I received a pleasant surprise: The government declared an automatic raise in rank to specific servicemen if they had performed specified duties. I qualified and suddenly I was a captain.

Two years in hospitals eventually became a bore and challenged my patience, even though much of the time I did my healing at home on leave, wearing a cast or brace and using crutches or a cane. The hospitals needed my bed for other wounded servicemen being evacuated from the war. When the doctors finally told me that they knew of no proven remedy for my problem at that time (1947), I was resigned to taking a medical discharge -- and a pension. I left the Air Force in February of 1947 with the intention of investigating civilian medicine for help for my knee. I obtained writing and editing jobs in journalism that minimized pressure on my legs.

In 1982 I had my left knee replaced, and it still works in 2012. In the late 1980s my right knee and right hip started aching and failing as a result of the extra work they did to compensate for the weakness of the left leg. Doctors warned me to have the two joints replaced while the scraping bones were still in good enough condition to withstand replacement. I followed their advice, but seven years later the joints produce frequent imbalance and pain.

With the addition of a pacemaker for my heart, my friends call me a bionic man.

After his discharge Pete returned to Cornell, starting in summer school. There he met Jane Anderson, a Wellesley College student who was at Cornell just for the summer. They both graduated from their respective schools in 1949 and were married in September of that year. They settled in New York while Pete earned an MS degree at Columbia's Graduate School of Journalism. They moved to Buffalo, Pete's home town, where he began a journalism career with United Press (later renamed United Press International, or UPI). In 1955 he was transferred to UPI's headquarters in New York and assigned to the foreign news department. While there he earned an MA in foreign affairs at Columbia. After 12 years he moved to The New York Times for another twelve years as a writer/editor for the Sunday "Week in Review" section. In 1977 he was invited to join the faculty of Columbia's School of Journalism and thirteen years later he switched to the School of International and Public Affairs (SIPA) where he directed the International Media and Communications program until he retired from Columbia in 2008. Pete and Jane have five children, eight grandchildren and two great grandchildren. They came to Woodland Pond in January, 2010.

AN ARMY NURSE'S MEMORIES OF WORLD WAR II

Mida Kaelin

Unlike the experiences of the young men who fought and killed and were wounded or permanently disabled during World War II my experience as an army nurse was interesting and I enjoyed it. I had gained considerable experience as an operating room nurse before I joined the army so I was pleased to be assigned to the operating rooms no matter where I was sent.

Six weeks of basic training at a very basic camp apparently hastily built on a patch of prairie in Colorado introduced me to army life. Our living quarters consisted of a series of small rooms just large enough to hold a chest of drawers, two narrow cots, and not much else. There were no closets and the walls and ceiling were unfinished, leaving the 2 x 4's and insulation exposed. On a trip to Colorado Springs the next day I purchased a hammer and some nails to pound into the 2x4s so that we could hang up our clothes and the small mirror my roommate bought, and our room was then habitable.

Every morning before breakfast we assembled in a large room where a nimble young woman with a beautiful figure led us through beneficial exercises to keep us fit. After breakfast a sergeant worked with us for an hour trying to teach us to march in an orderly manner. This was hard for me because no matter whether he ordered us to turn left or right I always turned right. Finally he ordered me to put a rock in my left shoe to help me remember that I had a left side. The rest of the day was spent listening to lectures and participating in practical demonstrations such as how to put up a tent or how to tie useful knots.

On the last day, full of information, we waited excitedly for our first orders which would tell us where we were being sent. I was hoping for orders to go overseas, perhaps to a temporary hospital close to a battlefield where wounded soldiers could be treated quickly, but I was destined to be disappointed. My first assignment was to report to the operating room supervisor at Fitzsimmons Hospital in Aurora, Colorado, a suburb of Denver. It was just a large army hospital surrounded by several acres of green lawn with an officers' club and some permanent housing on one edge of the lawn. By the time I arrived the lawn had been covered by new buildings to house the extra doctors and nurses and other new workers. There was also a chapel, a movie theater, a large general store called the Post Exchange, a restaurant with a small dance floor, a club house for nurses and a clubhouse for GIs and WACs (Women's Army Corps). In short, it had become a small village where almost everyone could find something to do while off duty, and I quickly forgot my disappointment. I spent almost two years there until the war in Japan ended and I got orders to go to a large general hospital in Tokyo, which turned out to be the most interesting part of my army career.

To get to Japan I was transported with ninety-nine other nurses on a troop ship. Bunk beds had been placed side by side and filled a large area where we sat, slept, read and played cards. To get exercise we could leave our beds and take a walk on the deck. We crossed the international dateline on my birthday, which meant that we had two May 20ths in a row. Some friends helped me celebrate both birthdays. The birthday "cakes" were a large sweet roll with a tampon stuck in the middle as a candle which we did not try to light.

When we landed in Yokohama my first surprise was being greeted by a polite, friendly smile on any Japanese person we encountered. Politeness I could understand, but not all of that willingness to be friendly with their recent American enemies. I know that the Americans they captured during the war were not greeted with smiles. The Japanese were often cruel captors. Furthermore, we had dropped nuclear bombs on two of their cities and done considerable damage with ordinary bombs, imprisoned and were executing some of their leaders and had occupied the country and taken over the government. Even if they remembered that they had begun the war they should surely be feeling resentful but, if that was the case, they were very good at concealing their feelings. It puzzled me. After the Japanese bombed Pearl Harbor we hated "The Japs", of course, but I found myself liking most of them while I was in Japan. Their friendly manner and willingness to please made them easy to work with.

Our bombs had made a shambles of Yokohama. As we drove through it on our way to Tokyo there was nothing to see but piles of shattered boards on each side of the road. The air had an unpleasant smell of rotting raw meat that added to the desolation and made me wonder if there could still be dead bodies under these boards. However, it was not dead bodies polluting the atmosphere. The smell was equally noticeable in Tokyo. A few days later I had an opportunity to ride into the countryside. I hoped to have a chance to breathe some fresh air but the smell there was overwhelming. The Japanese were not wasteful so they used human fecal material to fertilize their fields. Most of it was collected in Tokyo in large wooden buckets and placed in a row on long narrow carts to be hauled out of the city. They were a common site on the streets of Tokyo and the soldiers dubbed them "Honey Buckets". After a while I got accustomed to the scent and ceased to notice it.

When we got away from Tokyo one weekend I learned that the absence of resentment that puzzled me was not absent in several pretty small towns a few of us decided to visit. When we got out to walk around we were tolerated but no one wanted to speak to us and we were stared at with obvious dislike. In the last village, not so pretty, where the inhabitants appeared to be poorer, two men appeared and seemed to be asking for something. We could not understand them since they spoke in Japanese. When we failed to respond and began to walk away two more men joined them, and the four of them stared at us with such threatening expressions that we decided not to linger. They followed us back to our jeeps but didn't attack us and we were happy to get back to the smiling Japanese citizens of Tokyo.

The Americans employed many Japanese workers. They were efficient and hard working and had one work habit that always amazed me. They seemed to think that any job that needed to be done could be done best by two people and when possible they worked in pairs. I watched two of them wrap and tie up a small box without getting in each other's way.

There was always something new to see and do in Japan and for young army nurses the social life was excellent too. The depressing things were the injured soldiers who could often not be helped greatly even by the most skillful surgeons, and the great waste and inefficiency that seems to be unavoidable in the armed services. Sometimes a war might be necessary but I left the army convinced that war is more likely to create more problems than it solves, and nothing has happened since then to alter my opinion.

I was born in 1917 in Eldon, MO. Two years later my parents moved to Laramie, WY where we lived on a ranch for five or six years. I have many happy memories of that period. In 1930 we moved back to Eldon. The Great Depression had begun. My father, who built houses, discovered that not many persons at that time wanted to buy a new house. Hard times followed and there was no money for me to go to college. Marriage or an eventual career as a teacher, secretary or nurse were the main choices available to young women at that time. I chose nursing and took my training at the Deaconess Hospital in St. Louis, followed by the Mayo Clinic in Rochester, MN where I specialized in Operating Room Nursing. I then returned to the Deaconess Hospital to spend two years as operating room supervisor before going in the Army Nurse Corp.

In 1947 I left the army to marry Robert Kaelin, whom I met in the army. We had a son and daughter. When they reached school age I went to work at the Benedictine Hospital in Kingston as a clinical instructor in OR nursing. I retired at fifty but soon realized that I would like to work part time. I was offered a job as full time Operating Room Supervisor at the VA hospital in Castle Point, NY where I worked until I was 65.

Retirement often means that you simply get busy doing something else. My husband and I enjoyed our busy retirement until he became ill and died in 2008. I moved to Woodland Pond in 2009.

MY MILITARY LIFE

Pat Kirkpatrick

Pat and Grace Kirkpatrick 1952

World War II (for the U.S.A.) ran its course while I was in high school. I turned seventeen after graduating and my mom agreed to give her permission, allowing me to enlist in the U.S. Army Air Corps. My druthers were to pursue education. I would need to become a Certified Public Accountant (CPA) but family finances being what they were, that wasn't a realistic option.

As I was going through the Army induction process I was quickly introduced to a sample of what military life would be like. There were about fifty of us going through the procedures preliminary to being sworn in (this included a physical exam, extensive interviews and a six page form with all sorts of details about medical history, education, etc.) when the M/Sgt in charge of this event called out in a loud and gruff voice, "Who the hell is Do Ro Ko?" I have always used a small 'o' for my periods and to dot my i's. A few places on the lengthy form I was required to affix my initials. Upon confessing that I was Do Ro Ko I was told in no uncertain terms to "Do the form over and do it right." Welcome to the Army!

I was offered my choice of training schools, but accounting options were not included. I chose Airborne Radio Operator Mechanic which I was granted and spent several months at Scott Field, Belleville, IL. Upon completion of training I was asked which geographical area I preferred. Europe was my first choice and South America was my second choice.

My travel to Japan was via the USS Hodges. I disembarked in Yokohama, spent two weeks in transient quarters in downtown Yokohama, then aboard another U.S. transport ship was sent to Manila, then a 50 mile trip through the jungle in an army truck to Clark Field in the Philippines. I spent two weeks there, and then returned via air to Johnson Field just outside of Tokyo. It was nearly three months from the time I left Scott Field until I arrived at Johnson Field. This would suggest that my presence wasn't urgently required.

At Johnson I was doing radio related work, but not as an airborne operator. I requested transfer to Haneda Field, also just outside of Tokyo. There they did have the need for my skills, and I was reassigned. This move also carried a financial advantage since flying duty included a 50% pay increase for the month. With cigarettes costing 50 cents a carton in the PX, and being a smoker at the time, I needed the money.

The mission of the squadron was to provide transport for VIPS in "occupied" Japan. We had a few cargo planes, C-47s, several B-17s and MacArthur's privately assigned C-54 (named Bataan). All of these aircraft had been reconditioned to better serve their new role. The B-17s, for example, had all gunner sections removed, the bomb bays equipped with extra fuel tanks and the main interior fitted with a mini galley and a plush living area with a sofa and a table between two facing overstuffed chairs. The radio operator had a seat with table and radios in a compartment between the plush area and the bomb bays.

During one of our 'missions', transporting a general, we encountered some severe weather and hit an air pocket causing us to drop suddenly, probably 100 or so feet. Unfortunately the general had just been given a cup of coffee. The general and his cup became airborne for a few seconds and then dropped suddenly, but the coffee itself was captured by the ceiling and then dripped on the general who was on the floor. I think he said a bad word. Luckily, I had no coffee and my legs under my table kept me well seated.

Travelling to various places in the far Pacific was good duty and I enjoyed it sufficiently that I was easy to talk into re-upping for another three year hitch. The inducement included a bonus of $360, a rather significant amount in 1949. All went well and I was looking forward to returning to the U.S. of A. in July of 1950. Things sometimes are altered by the fickle finger of "hate."

While golfing on a nearby course on Sunday morning on June 25, 1950, a Japanese worker came by and told us that we were assigned to Tachikawa Air Base; we were instructed to immediately return there. Being assigned to Haneda Air Base (note: all members of the Army Air Corps had been transferred to the newly designated Air Force and Fields were now called Air Force Bases), I continued my golf without knowing what was up. As I found out, upon returning to Haneda, the Korean War (Police Action) had started. That caused Truman to extend enlistments by one year and to freeze transfers of anyone out of Japan who had a critical MOS (Military Occupation Specialty), and of course, mine was one of those.

During my extended stay in Japan our entire squadron was kept very busy ferrying generals and admirals from place to place within the Pacific theater of operations. One most memorable flight I participated in took place in early September 1950. Typically our flights were to transport some individual(s) to and /or from someplace. We also typically followed existing airways that were marked with beacons (where ground was available) to facilitate navigation. The flight of exception was one from Tokyo to an air base in South Korea. This in itself was not unusual, but to fly direct, almost due west, passing near Mt. Fujiyama (elevation 12,400 feet) was. We also had no passengers going and none returning. Upon landing in South Korea we were met by a jeep that gave us two very large reels of film and we immediately turned around and returned directly to Tokyo. A staff car met us upon arrival, took the reels of film, and our flight was over. About three days later (September 15, 1950) the Inchon Invasion took place. Until proven otherwise I will assume our cargo on that flight played a significant role in that historic event.

Finally, I was relieved of my contributions to the Korea War and returned to the U.S.A. in the summer of 1951. One of our squadron aircraft was due for a major overhaul and I was able to return home as the operator on that flight and thereby avoid a not-so-pleasant ride on a transport ship.

Unbeknownst to me at the time, in May of 1951, Grace Groves joined the Air Force at the age of 21, mostly to get away from farm life in Ohio. She was sent to Scott Air Force Base and given a brief introductory course in radio operation. This training allowed her to pre-flight aircraft radios to ensure they were operating correctly prior to flight. A never-ending chore. She was then transferred to Otis AFB on Cape Cod to perform that role until eligible for discharge in July 1953.

I was assigned to Otis in December 1951 and was made assistant radio shop leader. Grace's job came under my section and in rather short order we were dating. Shortly later Grace was transferred out of my section and served in an administrative capacity in the aircraft maintenance group, housed within the same building as the radio shop, but no direct link of responsibility. This worked fine for both of us and it came to pass that we were married in September 1952.

My Truman year was to terminate in June 1953 at which time I was going to take a two year course in radio and television engineering. Grace would be free to resign from the Air Force in July so our ducks were lined up very suitably. Then a complication arose. Truman, in late 1952, shortened his one year extension and I was to be discharged within two weeks. Grace however would not be available for several months. Fortunately for us, we had learned a week earlier that Grace was pregnant and, with the assistance of the Base Chaplain, were able to expedite some slightly complicated procedures and Grace and I were both discharged on January 13, 1953.

That completed my experience with the military except for two items. First, The Bill of Rights provided funds that I was lacking six years earlier to continue my education. Second, our first son was born, courtesy of the military medical facilities at Selfridge AFB in Mt. Clemens, Michigan - not very far from where I was going to school.

So I didn't become a CPA, but my military experience and the support funding for continued education gave me enough background to do rather well with IBM for thirty-five years in the field of computers.

As you may have observed from reading the above, my military experience was a lark in the park compared to what many others went thru during the same time period. I was isolated from the true horrors of war. It was later in life, through extensive reading that the truth of the words, "War is Hell!" became real.

During Pat's thirty-five years with IBM the family grew to include two sons and a daughter. Each of the three married and the Pat/Grace tribe now includes six grandchildren. The thirty-five years with IBM included a number of relocations - Michigan to Massachusetts to New York to North Dakota to Iowa to Maryland to New Jersey and retirement in New York in 1990.

Grace and Pat traveled extensively after his retirement. The more notable of their travels included a nine week tour of New Zealand, Australia and Hawaii.

Grace suffered a severe stroke early in 2000 and that ended their travel. Pat was able to provide needed care for Grace in their home in Poughkeepsie, New York. Pat had a heart operation in 2007 that kept him in the hospital for three weeks and home recovery for another four weeks. Their three kids, each having their own family to care for, came to New York to care for Grace until Pat could handle things on his own. It was then that they planned a move to Woodland Pond at New Paltz to ease future demands on the other members of the family. Grace died in December 2011 due to cancer. Pat remains at Woodland Pond.

THE WRONG HAMMOCK

Janet K. Kissinger, in memory of her brother, Kenneth Kline

The Kline family

My brother survived one of the worst sea disasters of World War ll. On Christmas Eve 1944 my brother, Ken, was on the Belgian transport ship *SS Leopoldville* in the English Channel near Cherbourg. Many soldiers were on deck and many were below in hammocks, trying to relax or sleep. About 6 pm Ken went below and found someone else in his hammock.

When he told his fellow soldier that he was in the wrong hammock the soldier told Ken to sleep in his hammock, which was near a port hole. Ken, not wanting to create a scene, went to the other soldier's hammock.

A German U-boat was hiding below the surface and a torpedo struck the ship. Many men in some of the compartments were never seen again. Ken was trapped with debris that had fallen on his chest and legs. After he freed himself from this debris he swam through the port hole and reached the surface of the water in the nick of time. Fortunately someone on deck spotted him and pulled him to safety. We were told that Ken was given morphine and remained on the deck until a small boat came to rescue those that were hurt. When Ken was thrown from the SS *Leopoldville* to this small craft, the person in the craft barely caught him. Ken could have easily been thrown into the English Channel.

He spent time in an English hospital recovering from his injuries. My parents received a letter from the U.S. Army informing them that my brother had been hurt in battle. My mother's biggest fear was that Ken had lost his eyesight. He had some broken bones and lost his hearing for some time but there were no problems with his eyesight.

Such joy when he was with us once again. I was seven years old when all this happened. There were 112 from his company who lost their lives. Ken was one of seven who survived from his company. At Arlington National Cemetery there is a monument honoring the 800 who died with the ship. My brother felt blessed to have survived this event. He was also blessed to have a long marriage and two great sons. Looking back, he thanked God many times for extending his life. My family also thanks God for extending his life. I was very fortunate to have a loving older brother who meant so much to me.

S.S. Leopoldville, photo courtesy of Mike Kemble

Kenneth was drafted before graduating from high school. After his military experience he earned his GED (General Educational Development), became a tool and die maker, and worked for Ford Motor Company as a machinist until retirement. He married, had two sons, and valued each day. The last time I saw him in Skilled Nursing I said, "You survived!"

TWO PIECES

Steffi Lauer

Steffi and Lothar with children Michael and Ruth

Berlin 1938

The school had been until a few months earlier quite close to home, a walk of fifteen minutes or less, a walk that took me under a cover of trees past our long block of cobbled street and serene apartment buildings -- huge apartments; two to a floor with flowered balconies and tall, wrought-iron fences and gates in front and an inner court at the back -- then a city block of Berlinerstrasse (a cinema, a corner ice-cream place, small clothing stores along the lines of boutiques, tracks & cables in the center of the street for trams), finally another long residential block to the school. The school had been an apartment building much like the one we lived in. It was a private Jewish school, created, after Hitler's regime began, not in a spirit of religious fervor but out of necessity. But the second half of 1938 was already a restless time, and things began--things had begun to change. The school had been moved to a building in another part of the city and now included all the grade levels. So at this point, on this November morning, my walk to school took probably about 40 minutes and took me along a heavily trafficked route, first for several blocks along Berlinerstrasse, blocks that were busier and more crowded than the single one I had grown used to, and then for the major stretch into the majestic, imperial, blow-ye-the-trumpets sort of breadth and length of the Kaiserallee. I trudged along with my satchel on my back and my eyes mostly on the pavement. On either side, there were walled mansions and villas well set back from the street and from each other.

Now comes the part that I don't want to write about. It whirs often through my mind, it replays itself, but I have spoken of it rarely (perhaps never in any detail to my children?) and written of it I think only once before, a few years ago in my non indexed journal; I would certainly not be able to locate the page or even the particular notebook for that entry. First the smell, the stinging in my throat, the sudden need to cough. It was only then that I looked up and saw across the street the familiar fat, domed outline of the Prinzregenten synagogue belching with grimy clouds of smoke and livid with flames. I had on occasion sat next to my mother in the gallery for women and children of that synagogue. It had a grand sweep of marbled stair flights leading to its main portals. The gallery inside was a finely molded, soft off-white and round like the dome overhead. But now, as I stopped to take in what was happening, ugly little noises erupted from the mushrooming smoke and the crackle of flames; I saw across the width of the avenue a gray and heaving reddish mass of collapse. Except for the sputtering noises of the ebbing fire (it must already have been burning for many hours when I happened by) the atmosphere was still. No crowd was gathered in front of the dying edifice. S.A. men in their yellow uniforms stood guard to prevent--what? Unrest, agitation, the spreading of the fire to adjacent properties--and people hurried by speechlessly but unsurprised. I, too, did not linger. An immense rush of adrenaline--I think honestly more from horror than fear--sent me on my way. It took me a while after that to piece things together. My father had been removed during that night by the Gestapo. My brother, unlike me, had been awakened by voices during the night and (also unlike me) was not sent to school the next day. My mother--what was required of her and how she coped in the weeks following; I will write about that another time. It took me years to understand that the events of that night came to be referred to as *Kristallnacht*.

Berlin, 1952

In the summer of 1951 or '52 my parents hustled me off to Berlin. They went there (by sea, not by air) to see their old friend Walter Rieck--one of several Oskar Schindler types that had operated cleverly and recklessly from attics and cellars in and around Berlin--and to see if possible one or two others and to examine, again if possible, my father's apartment buildings. They took me with them for the sole purpose of breaking up a relationship with someone I had met in the English department at Harvard. He was Jewish and close to obtaining his doctoral degree, and we both believed, but I think he more than I, that we were going to get married. My parents, however, had other ideas for me. On the ship, before we left New York Harbor, he gave me a copy of E. M. Forster's *Howard's End* (known largely today as a Merchant-Ivory film of considerable distinction). He had written a message to me in Italian on the flyleaf. I was still then as perhaps I am still now the person who drifts from one situation into another so, in spite of the youthful roiling, moiling, and misery to be expected in that circumstance, I submitted and my parents succeeded in trampling on that relationship, going about it, though, in their usual apparently absent-minded, debonair way, and Lothar and our kids and I myself can thank them for that summer in Berlin. I tramped all over a smallish area of West Berlin, trying to locate the street and the building in which I had lived as a child, but I could not. Berlin had been cleaned up, sort of, it was quiet and grey and subdued and rather left to itself, but no rebuilding had begun, and except for parts of the Kurfürstendamm, where we were staying, and some residential streets close to it, the city was still a mess of craters and barren spaces, walls without windows, an unforgiving disorientation without sign posts, and I did not find my home.

Besides Walter Rieck and his new family (he was eighty and the new family consisted of a youngish, lively, well turned out actress--a beauty in the typically tailored, Berlinese way--and their three-year-old princeling of a son), my parents saw Werner Glatzer and his wife--I remembered Werner--, my Dada, who had been our nanny until we started elementary school and got governesses instead, and a female pharmacist who had survived years in one of the concentration camps and had returned to live alone in Berlin because, as she said to my mother (and it was one of the few things that she said at all), she had to live somewhere. The pharmacist had been drained of affect. She spoke but only matter-of-factly and to the point. She appeared--and no doubt was--indifferent to us and apathetic. She was a short, non-descript, middle-aged person with dried out, dull skin and hair. Her lack of emphasis and her indifferent appearance and wooden behavior implied that she was too worn and numbed to go to the trouble of committing suicide. She had nothing to say. The other old friends were "real" Germans and were bursting with things to say. Werner's wife, a tall thin woman with dead hair, had lost her nails--the ends of her fingers were just skin overgrown with fungi--from living on weeds and grass when there was no more food obtainable. Dada received us, in the same fine house in Lichterfelde that she had owned of old, looking very much as I remembered her but not in her starched blue & white nanny's uniform. Her house, which she shared with her sister, was known for the excellent cultivation of its garden, and she served us at this reunion her own freshly baked cake pliant in the mouth with raisins and rum. My first memory of Dada is of her breasts swinging above me (in a crib I suppose) as she rubs herself dry after washing. With Walter and his new family, we sat in one café after another all along the Kurfürstendamm or "Kuh-damm" (that's cow) as the Amis, the American soldiers, called it. Walter Rieck was a big man with a beer belly, a splendid head of silver-white hair, grandiose gestures, and handsome features softly wrinkled with age and swollen with beer. He had managed (or mismanaged, be that as it may) my father's properties during the war. He was a raconteur and liked to interrupt whoever was speaking by raising one arm and declaring, "Just one moment, please!" and then charging into the narrative of one of his wartime exploits, how he together with a blind partner (I don't mean a sleeping or silent partner; I mean a man who was blind) stayed on top of apartment tenants' vacation schedules and moved people who were in hiding continuously from one empty apartment into another, "and so on and so forth," as he liked to say before interrupting the next person with the narration of yet another escapade. I hung on his words, but my mother said she did not believe any of it. Many years later, in the 1980s, I came across a book, a memoir, in the public library that vindicated Walter's stories and claims. It was written by a woman who had been kept for years in hiding with her mother in Berlin and Potsdam thanks to the persistence and care and enterprise and risks taken by Walter and his associates. One afternoon, the five of us (or six if the little prince was there, too) were sipping coffee inside the restaurant of the Hotel Kempinsky. I say inside because on most days we sat outdoors, so it might have been raining on that occasion or it might have been after dark (unlikely, though, considering the very long dusk of the midsummer nights in northern Germany). Before the war, the Hotel Kempinsky had belonged to the family of one of my classmates, Karen Kutschera; the spelling is almost certainly wrong. Karen was a wild child who lived with her handsome brother on a farm outside Berlin and so had to travel a considerable distance each day to get to school. In fact, she and her brother were delivered every morning by one of the trucks from their farm. She was a lax student, a tomboy who drummed her fingers on the desk, twisted her silky but uncombed hair around her forefinger, wriggled almost continuously, and paid no particular attention to the teachers, but she was an excellent pianist, considered not quite as outstanding as another classmate, André Previn, but nearly so. Her playing was more tempestuous and more expressive than his but less polished and less accurate. A small orchestra was fiddling away while Walter and

Charlottchen and my parents and I sipped and sat and talked when, except for the sounds of music, a silence insinuated itself over the scattered drinkers and diners. My mother became ashen. The orchestra was playing the *Kol Nidre* score composed by Max Bruch.

Steffi graduated from Smith College with honors and received an M.A. with distinction from Harvard after which she taught college English until marrying James Lothar Lauer. While raising two children she continued writing and painting. Knopf published her novel, Home is the Place, *in 1957 and Steffi is a fellow of the Breadloaf Writers' Conference. Her husband died in 2008 and she moved to Woodland Pond in 2010 where she continues writing. Since 2001, in addition to* Dipping, *a full-length memoir, Steffi has written a short novel,* Art and Love, *two pieces of novella length and several stories*

Smith College

TRAGIC IRONY

Roger Leonard

Gary Leonard 1944

Harold Mattson 1944

My family lived in Old Tappan, NJ during World War ll. It was one mile from the West Shore Railroad, and I could hear the mournful whistle of the trains as I lay in bed by my open window. One night in September, 1944 when I was nine years old I was listening more expectantly than usual. We were waiting for a phone call from my cousin Betty's new husband, Harold. They had recently married in Chicago where my mother's family lived. Now as Harold, the pilot of a B-17, was about to ship out, my parents had invited them to our home for their last week together. I remember hearing the train come in. In minutes our phone rang. It was Harold, and I was permitted to come down to the kitchen to meet and welcome him. He was tall, slim, blond, as was my cousin Betty.

For a week they spent most days seeing the sites in the city, but he found the time to buy a model airplane kit and meticulously put it together at a card table in our living room. Soon the short visit was over. As he left he gave me a pin, his "pilot's wings", as he had a new set of his own

I also had a cousin Garry (Garrison), the son of my Uncle Irving and Aunt Milly, who had also joined the Army Air Corps and become a navigator on a B-17. Garry was someone I admired very much. He and his family lived a short distance away in New Milford. He was ten years older than I and did not think it beneath him to play games with me. The town tennis court bordered their home and he would take his model airplane out there and let me wind up the propeller, release it, and watch it struggle into the air.

That fall of 1944 Thanksgiving was at Aunt Bess' and Uncle Bill's in nearby Harrington Park. As usual most of the family was there except for the cousins away at war. Garry was soon to ship out. The rest of us ate and visited. Then the stand up telephone by the dining room window rang. It was Garry, calling to wish everyone a Happy Thanksgiving. We all lined up, so happy to talk to him.

In early January we received a letter from Harold:

Dec. 44 England

Dear Eunice & All,

I'm doing a pretty fair job of catching up on all of my letter writing this evening. You might say I was cleaning house so as to start out the year of forty-five in grand style. So far I've written five letters and yours is the sixth. No, that doesn't include one to Betty either. I didn't have a very nice Christmas this year for we had a little bad luck. We went over and gave the Germans a Christmas present and when we came back our field was closed in because of weather. As a result of this we had to land at another field. We spent Christmas Eve in our airplane for we had to sleep there. We fared better the following day, however, for we did get our Christmas turkey.

I've got 14 missions to my credit now so a mere 21 more and I'll be through (ha ha). That seems a long ways off but if everything goes all right and we get good flying weather it should easily finish up in three months at the rate I'm going now. The recent ones I've gone on have been fairly easy with hardly any flak to speak of. If they would only continue that way it would be all right but luck can't last and they will start getting rougher for awhile.

I'm so tired when I get back from a raid that I don't feel much like writing letters and if I do have any energy left I always write to Betty. Sometimes when we fly one raid after another, or at least get up for one before it's scrubbed because of weather, we get pretty edgy and nervous. Nothing like sleep to revive a man.

I hope you had a nice Christmas and saw the New Year come in with a bang. Not much else to write so I'll close.

Love, Harold

Mom had us all sit right down and write to Harold.

Soon we heard that Garry had been assigned to his Flying Fortress B-17 and crew in Tenn. On January 7th they left for England, arriving on the 17th. We heard that every crew flew a northern route to England on their own plane, making frequent stops along the way, being over water as little as possible.

Early in February I came home from school and Mom had heart sinking news. Betty's mother had written that they had received word that Harold was declared "missing in action". That night as I lay in bed I looked up at the model airplane Harold had made for me, hanging from the ceiling light fixture in my bedroom. I listened for the night train. I wished Harold would be on it and that I would hear the phone ring to tell us he was down at the station. Later Betty received a letter from the government asking if she wanted his body brought home. She said she didn't know they found him. He was the pilot. He saw that everyone was safely out, but it was too late for him to parachute to safety. The plane crashed, but apparently a body was found. She did not choose to have his body brought home.

About a week after hearing of Harold's loss my Aunt Stella and her daughter Margie were visiting us. They had come on their own little trip from Chicago. It was a Saturday and we were all sitting and visiting in our living room. Regal Aunt Stella sat very erect with her white upsweep hairdo, elegantly smoking a cigarette. Mom said she was "stately". Eleven-year-old Margie sat by the fireplace, her face buried in a comic book. Mom, Pop and Meryl were all sitting there chatting pleasantly. I was just listening. The phone rang. Pop slipped through the drapes that separated the hallway and the cold from the living room to save fuel.

"Oh yes, Bill." We realized it was Uncle Bill. Uncle Bill hardly ever called. Pop's tone changed from cheer to a very grave one. Mom knew at once. Mom always knew. She gasped, "It's Garry." Pop hung up the phone and came back through the drapes. "That was Bill." In silence we all stared at him. "Garry was killed." Shock slammed into the room. Mom choked out, "What happened?" "He doesn't know much about it. Irving called him. They received a telegram this morning. It said he was killed in action over France. That's all he knows." He said he could hear Millie crying in the background.

Meryl got up and ran upstairs. I sat there unable to move or ask or say anything. I felt numb. I looked over at Margie. The comic book was very close to her face, but I could see big tears welling in her eyes and streaming down her cheeks. Aunt Stella said, "I need a cup of coffee." Mom, Pop and Aunt Stella continued to talk as they went into the kitchen.

Margie went out the back door into the yard. I went up to my bedroom. Garry. Garry killed. "Killed". The word took on new meaning. Just like Harold. They were killed. The word "killed" is such a terrible word. It was so shocking. How could it be? And each in a B-17. A Flying Fortress.

Mom and Pop said we were going over to see Aunt Milly, Uncle Irving and Garry's sister, Marion. Their house was filled with people. Marion greeted us at the door, her eyes red with grief. Aunt Milly was sitting in the dining room surrounded by women friends. Uncle Irving was in his chair in front of the stairway next to the big console radio. He got up and shook Pop's and my hands. He slumped back into his chair shaking his head over and over. Some of his friends were trying to get him to talk about hunting and fishing. He said, "I don't want to talk about hunting. I want to talk about my boy."

There was talking and weeping. Aunt Milly told us that all of her life she anticipated letters before they arrived and knew when they were coming and from whom. But this telegram she never expected. "My boy, my boy," she cried. She knew the minute she looked out the door and saw the Western Union man standing there. She said she screamed. Marion showed each of us the telegram. Later Uncle Irving said that he had looked in his diary. Garry was killed on February sixth, the night Aunt Milly and Uncle Irving had seen the movie, *Wings of Victory*.

There would be no funeral. They had decided not to have Garry's body brought home. He would be buried in a military cemetery near Epinal, France where it happened. We didn't hear the particulars at the time of how it happened, but in the weeks to come we learned that it was Garry's first mission. The planes had not even reached enemy lines. As they flew their B-17 Flying Fortress in formation the plane above Garry's, for some reason, came down on top of them and damaged their plane making it impossible to fly. We learned that the pilot gave the orders to abandon the plane and that all were able to get out except Garry, the navigator.

Sixty-seven years later, in the spring of 2012, my wife Bernice and I finally stood at Garry's grave at the Epinal American Cemetery and Memorial in Epinal, France.

Roger grew up in Old Tappan, New Jersey. He graduated from Hope College, Holland, Michigan and earned his M.Div. from New Brunswick Theological

Seminary, in New Jersey. He is an ordained minister in the Reformed Church in America. Roger began his ministry in the New Paltz Reformed Church where he met and married his wife, Bernice. They moved to Red Hook, New York, where he served as pastor of St. John's Reformed Church for almost thirty-three years. It was there that their children Kathy, Doug, and Greg were born and raised. Roger then served as an Area Minister for the Synod of New York for seven years. In addition to his recent history, Upper Red Hook: An American Crossroad, *Roger also wrote a history of the mother church of St. John's, titled,* The Red Church. *Roger and Bernice now reside at Woodland* Pond.

Roger at Epinal
Military Cemetery
visiting his cousin's
grave

SQUADRON SURGEON

Paul R. Lurie, MD

It sounds like a romantic wartime idyll. The reality is quite boring, but typical of many roles that had to be filled in the vast war machine that had suddenly blossomed from a small peace-time seed.

I had finished an internship in pediatrics at the end of June, 1943, and was immediately inducted into the Air Force. My first year was spent acting as a psychiatrist at the Station Hospital, Drew Field, Tampa, Florida. This was a rest and reassignment station for radar operators who were back from exotic assignments, often isolated from any personal contact for months in places like the Aleutians and Guadalcanal. All most of the guys wanted was to be declared physically unfit for further service. To distinguish real disease (today called PTSD) from malingering became nearly impossible and, under the direction of the psychiatrist who was my mentor, I signed Certificates of Disability Discharge for dozens of radar men. That experience taught me that I was not cut out to be a psychiatrist.

The headquarters of 3rd Fighter Command was across the street from the hospital and one day I got orders to report over there for my new assignment. The Chief Surgeon of the command was an aging cardiologist whom I got to know much better years later in peacetime. Very seriously he told me to start reading the comic strip "Terry and the Pirates" as that gave a pretty realistic story of what The Air Commandos were doing and I was being assigned to a similar outfit. The group had an assortment of aircraft designed to support the ground troops who were pushing the Burma Road through the jungle into China in order to avoid having to fly over the perilous "hump" -- the Himalayas. We, the 2nd Air Commandos, were to be trained to follow their footsteps as soon as possible.

The planes included P51 fighters, L5s (little 2-seat liaison planes), troop-carrying gliders, and C47 transports. Where would I fit in? An airdrome squadron or two were necessary to house and support all of these people except the pilots. They were cared for and coddled by flight surgeons with special training. I was to be Squadron Surgeon, 327th Airdrome Squadron. It was already a bit less romantic!

The subsequent months were spent in various Florida air stations. I was able for a time to do a physical exam and include a mental status form of my own devising that enabled me to reject a few of the worst risk recruits from entry into our organization. Higher HQ soon got wind of this and put an end to my efforts at psychiatric screening. Some interesting events occurred in those Florida months. A hurricane hit our base. All personnel were ordered to shelter in a local high school gym. Wives were left out. Luckily, my wife did well in our rented apartment but a few buildings in the nearby town were ruined.

In addition to lots of routine flight activity I saw large transport gliders full of dummies snatched off the ground by C47s, a sight I will never forget. One day I was told to get into an ambulance that had been assigned to search the scene of a B17 Flying Fortress training crash in the nearby Florida jungle. For the first time in all of my medical experience I was introduced to the characteristic odor of burnt human flesh. We found no survivors.

I got to know intimately my small medical detachment, a staff sergeant, corporal and two privates. We conducted sick call each morning, inspected the latrines and the mess each day and that was about all we did. We learned how to spend time. We had lots of books. We played chess. We took lots of naps. This pattern was followed on the 30-day voyage to Bombay on the General John Pope, owned by the army but run by naval officers and routed very far south to avoid the Japanese Navy.

The routine continued as we were based first in India in a region of small villages and rice paddies west of Calcutta, and later on the eastern shore of the Bay of Bengal at the southernmost tip of India, now Bangladesh. We were just over a mountain from Burma. It was an idyllic place. On the ocean side there was about a quarter-mile wide expanse of hard-packed sand that served as runway for our planes. Up from that was the grassy flat for our encampment. Next came the jungle, rising abruptly into the spiky mountain range, the Arakan Yoma.

There was a tiny nearby village named Cox's Bazar. It was just a few grass huts and a dozen or so colorful market tables in the open air. The locals wore garments that seemed more Burmese than Indian. We were not encouraged to fraternize with the natives and did not. There was an exception. One of our enlisted men got himself shot because of making advances on some man's spouse. Another surgeon treated him and sent him off to a hospital.

Let me say a word about sick call. I diagnosed and directed but did little hands-on treatment as I had so much more help than was actually necessary. Fungus infections, athlete's foot and jock itch were the most common problems. We treated them with local application of either Gentian Violet or Castellani's Paint, a mixture of resorcinol and a brilliant red dye. We used liters of both. There were sporadic cases of gastroenteritis, mostly diarrhea, but no mass epidemics, perhaps because our food was entirely out of cans or boxes, nothing at all local. We used a lot of kaopectate and paregoric. Everyone took routine preventive dosage of atebrine and slept with individual mosquito bars so I never treated a single case of malaria. Happily, there were NO war wounds. Our base was never under attack. Though we had foxholes just outside our basha, we used them only for a few drills. A Japanese observation plane came over once but quickly withdrew.

One afternoon in beautiful weather one of the L5 pilots whom I had gotten to know took me on a "training flight" over the Arakan into Burma. We looked around the jungle scene, turned around without landing and came back for we had been warned that there still were some Japanese holdouts in the area.

The top of the CBI brass was Lord Louis Mountbatten, a member of the British royal family. One day a cabin plane of unfamiliar style landed right in front of us. Mountbatten and his Lady came down the gangplank and were whisked away in a command car. I was only about 150 yards away from all that rank. If only one of them had needed medical attention! Years later I read that the Lady was then having an affair with Pandit Nehru.

One other interesting event occurred to break the monotony of our existence at Cox's Bazar. Our squadron intelligence officer got to know the commander of the Royal Garhwali Lancers and we five officers of the 327th were invited to his encampment nearby for dinner one evening. He was a young bank officer from a town in the Midlands of England who had been sent out to India before the war started to singlehandedly organize and train a company of ground troops from the mountainous province of Garhwal. Here he was with a heavily armed group of Indian fighters now in rest camp awaiting reassignment. They had chosen a location on one side of a deep gully. Everything was organized around the gully with their quarters, mess, and weapons on this side and their targets over there. As their guests, after supper we were expected to indulge in shooting a variety of weapons ranging from pistols to submachine guns and finally to their Browning automatic rifle, a huge thing shooting .30 caliber bullets. Medical officers did not have many opportunities to shoot anything, so I tried them all. Despite the rum that went into the strong tea I enjoyed the whole thing and even hit some bulls' eyes.

After a few months I got a call from American Red Cross. My younger brother, who had kidney disease, had died, my dad was near death from a stroke and a heart attack and my mother was in bad shape. My duties were taken over by another squadron surgeon. I was able to hitch a flight home on a transport plane that stopped in Karachi, Cairo, and Casablanca, each time stopping long enough for me to take in some of the local sights. I took a taxi to the pyramids and sphinx, saw them and immediately turned around and came back. I just didn't think the pilot would wait for me if I was late.

I was reassigned to an air base near home and did what I could to help my mother before and after Dad's death. Then I worked in a series of airbase station hospitals awaiting a call to go to Japan as part of the invasion we all expected. It never happened. "The Bomb" was dropped, there was VJ Day and soon there was discharge. I returned to Yale and finished my pediatric training. The three years in the service had been uneventful.

Paul is a retired pediatric cardiologist, a medical specialty that was just emerging as he completed three years service as a medical officer in World War II. "I was lucky to fall into it as one of the pioneers," he says. Born in Amsterdam, NY. Paul graduated from Harvard and Columbia Medical School, and did his internship and residency in pediatrics at Yale. In his second year at Harvard, the police arrested Paul and six other students for distributing handbills in support of labor unions at a factory gate without a permit. The judge deemed their action both legal and laudable, and proposed a plea of nolo contendere. These young idealists accepted the plea bargain, and the judge promptly released them.

Paul's decision to pursue pediatric cardiology took him to Indiana's James Whitcomb Hospital for Children for seventeen years, then to University of Southern California's Children's Hospital of Los Angeles for fifteen years. He retired in 1982 to Albany Medical College where he continued research, teaching and writing. After his wife's death Paul came to Woodland Pond in 2011

MY BROTHER ROBERT

W. Robert Shimer, Jr.

as remembered and assembled by his sister, Margaret MacDowell

Kid sisters are totally involved with big brothers. Many years ago Robert told me, in a semi-stern manner, "Only my friends may call me Bob." I accepted that statement without hesitation. After all, it was the LAW of the BROTHER.

His favorite ploy, which only I could fall for: Scene: Brother preparing to go on a date. Kid sister, standing by, envious of his superior years. Brother: "Hey, kid, how about it, wanna earn a nickel?" "Sure," replies kid sister. Big brother says, "Polish my shoes and the nickel is yours." Eager to please, I get to it... Ten minutes later, fingers stained with cordovan polish, kid sister deposits shoes at brother's closed door. "Thanks, I'll pay you later, I don't have time right now," comes the deep voice from beyond. Stupid sister replies, "Ok." Years later I remembered the often repeated scene. "Hey Robert, you owe me a ton of money." "Oh yeah, what's the deal?" "Shoe polishing plus thirty-five years interest." "Ha ha ha ha" is all I got. I was a pretty stupid kid, that has got to be the truth, and I loved every minute of it.

Robert attended Admiral Farragut Academy in Tom's River, NJ in 1936. One weekend my parents and I visited the school primarily to watch him take part in crew racing. He was in his dress whites, as were the rest of his mates. They were all so handsome, I mused, seeing them through the eyes of a thirteen-year-old who was at the stage in which maybe boys were not so terrible after all. I remember my white cotton dress with navy blue trim and a wide-brimmed white summer hat. I felt 'girly' and somewhat eager to meet those great looking older teens. How I would brag when he returned home! So my darling brother commenced to introduce me to two or three of his friends. "This is my sister, Peg," he speaks out. "She is a model!" Wowee, I say to myself, he is going to be nice today. Not quite finished with the introduction he continues, "She is the BEFORE in the BEFORE and AFTER pictures." Well, 'strangle' is not the word-'torture' would be more appropriate. It is a good thing he was not coming home with us that day; by the time he had a break I was over it.

Robert enlisted in the Navy in 1943 and was sent out of the country. We had no idea where he was located over those long months away. One day a letter arrived dated September, 1945, censorship lifted. He gave Dad a brief run-down of his activities: "I spent time in Kimming and Chungking...at headquarters in both cities...heading out of Chungking and going through Sawchow, Mingshaw to Upper Singapore Province near the Yellow River in Inner Mongolia, seventy-five miles from Jap lines…" He calmly stated, "We had several interesting experiences as a result of our stay here. The Japs moved some light tanks into the field against our forces and we had a fairly unpleasant time of it all around with poor food and a cholera epidemic. Conditions became especially bad when a reward of six million Chinese dollars was put on the head of each American captured, dead or alive. We had to depend upon small farmers and restaurants for our food and most of the time it became so dangerous that we had to enter towns in small, heavily armed groups. Fifty percent of the hostile troops in the area were puppet troops (Jap trained Chinese) so half the time we never knew whom to trust. We went to Paotow disguised as Chinese officers, but when we got there we changed in Japanese officers' uniforms. The enemy evidently did the same thing so that we often skirmished with groups with no assurance they were the enemy."

"There's a possibility that I may be able to return home fairly soon."

Well, needless to say, that was the best news ever!

Robert Shimer enlisted in the Navy in 1943 and was in active service until 1946. He was involved at the start of the early Frogmen training, forerunner of the Navy Seals which began in August, 1942 as the Scout/Raider concept. The third Scout and Raiders organization operated in China. They were deployed to fight with the Sino-American Cooperative Organization (SACO). Admiral Ernest J. King ordered one hundred twenty officers and nine hundred men trained for 'Amphibious Roger' at the Scout and Ranger school in Florida. They formed the core of what was envisioned as "guerrilla amphibious groups of Americans and Chinese operating from coastal waters, lakes and rivers employing small steamers and sampans." Three of the groups saw active service. They conducted a survey of the Upper Yangtze River in the spring of 1945 and, disguised as coolies, conducted a detailed three-month survey of the Chinese coast from Shanghai to Kitchioh Wan near Hong Kong.

Bob was awarded the Asiatic-Pacific Theater Campaign Medal, the American Theater Ribbon, and the WW II Victory Medal.

COUNTER INTELLIGENCE OFFICER WITH THE 101ST AIRBORNE

Frank Martini

"We knew where they were . . . in Berchtesgaden, the area 35 to 40 miles around Berchtesgaden. They were being captured by the soldiers and brought to us, the Counter Intelligence Corps, for processing. We would then interrogate them, arrest them and send them on to army headquarters. That's basically how we got them."

Born in 1920, Frank Martini grew up in Brooklyn and had just graduated from Brooklyn College in May 1942 when he was drafted into the Army. After basic training he went to military police school. This was followed by infantry officers' school at Ft. Benning, GA. Next came training in military intelligence.

In January 1945, Frank was shipped to France. He continues the story:

"I joined the 101st Airborne Division in Mormelon, France. At the time, I was a second lieutenant infantry and subsequently became a first lieutenant and head of the 101st's Counter Intelligence Corps detachment. We then crossed the Rhine into Germany and I was with them in combat phases from January to about April 10th or 12th 1945.

"At that point we started picking up high ranking Nazis. We had been arresting Nazis all the way from France into Germany to Berchtesgaden and now the reason we were getting higher ranking Nazis in Berchtesgaden was because at that time they were fleeing Berlin. The Russians had now encircled Berlin and were closing in on them. There was to be a last ditch struggle by the Germans at Berchtesgaden. That's where Hitler had his Eagle's Nest. It didn't come to anything though because they decided to call it quits. They were afraid of the Russians, with good reason. They were brutal to Russian civilians and soldiers during the war and fully expected to get the same treatment from the Russians if they were captured by them."

Frank and his unit set up shop in Berchtesgaden as initial interrogators of suspects brought in by members of the 101st, often aided by local informants. Among those interrogated were: Dr. Robert Ley, chief of the German Labor Front and founder of the Strength Through Joy movement; Franz Schwarz, treasurer of the Nazi Party; Paula Wolf, Hitler's sister; and Gertraud "Traudl" Junge, one of Hitler's secretaries.

Given their past activities, many of those arrested had equipped themselves for suicide should they be captured. Among the first to examine them at length after capture, Frank and his men had to be particularly vigilant.

A case in point was Dr. Ley. He was captured forty-five miles south of Berchtesgaden by two privates of the 502nd Parachute Regiment who were acting on a tip from a civilian. When found, the diminutive Ley (5 ft. 4 in.) was in a country house, wearing blue pajamas and a growth of beard. Complaining of a heart attack, he attempted to swallow a vial of poison. When he was examined by Lt. Martini and his men, they found razor blades secreted in the lapel of his coat. On October 24, 1945, three days after being indicted at Nuremburg for crimes against humanity, Ley strangled himself in his cell using a noose made of toweling, fastened to the toilet pipe in his cell.

After Germany surrendered on May 8, 1945, Frank recalled, "I was still Counter Intelligence. They were then going to form a unit to drop in on Japan. We were going to go to California, get training there then go to the Far East and on to Japan. Fortunately, we dropped the atomic bomb. I think it was August 6 and the war ended soon after.

"They deactivated the 101st Airborne and the whole division was supposed to come home. However, the Cold War was heating up so I was not with the division when it marched down Fifth Avenue in New York City. I had been sent to Berlin briefly and then back home the end of 1945."

Using the G.I. Bill, Frank went to New York Law School at night and worked during the day at an insurance company. When asked how he and Barbara met, he recounted:

"I was in law school and used to smoke a pipe all the time. I'd go to the library entrance to smoke my pipe. The librarian was a very assertive woman . . . probably my age or a little older. She said, 'You going to be here tomorrow? Be here! I've got a girl I want you to meet.' But then, we didn't get married for around four years.

"Jimmy Loeb, whom I'd been very friendly with overseas, had us up to his apartment one night. His wife told me, 'If you don't marry that girl, you're crazy.'" Barbara added, "They ganged up on him." In effect, Frank had two matchmakers working on his behalf.

In January 1951, Frank was called back into service for the Korean War. Because of his combat experience and having taught French and Italian as an undergraduate, "I became an instructor in interrogation techniques [at Fort Holabird, Baltimore, MD]. But nothing like what they did at Abu Ghraib. For very simple reasons: First, it shows disrespect for human beings and for the United States. Secondly, you don't get valid information. They'll tell you anything you want to hear. We taught them how to use better techniques to get true information."

After about a year of service Frank was discharged from the Army for good. "So then we went out West. I had a month's leave and a new car, a Ford."

Barbara added, "He had spent a great deal of his life in foreign countries so I thought he ought to see some of his own." It was time for the delayed honeymoon.

Among other souvenirs of his military service, Frank has the 1936 membership card to the Baden-Baden Internationaler Club held by Joachim von Ribbentrop, Hitler's Foreign Minister; his own place card at The Commanding General's Mess, 101st Airborne Division; and his 21 September 1944 War Department Identification Card. Its top line reads: "Not a Pass – For Indentification Only"

After graduation from law school and release from the military, Frank practiced law with a specialty in civil litigation with Dewitt, Nast, Diskin & Martini, which was dissolved in 1975. Frank then returned to litigation with an insurance company from which he retired in 1993. For a few years afterwards, he did courtroom work for other attorneys then retired completely. He and Barbara, an artist, made their home in

Brooklyn, where they raised two daughters and a son. After retirement, they moved to Buck Hill Falls, PA, until joining the Woodland Pond community in 2012.

Lt. Martini and Dr. Ley

Dr. Ley after capture

Ribbentrop Membership card

MERRILL'S MARAUDERS SURVIVOR

ALEX MINEWSKI

In 1931 unemployment hit 8 million and 2,500 banks in the United States failed. Alex Minewski was fourteen. He left home but stayed at Cass Technical High School in Detroit where he felt he received "a solid basic art background." Summers, he took his sketchbook west where he worked jobs at a carnival, a circus and as a sign painter and logger.

During the thirties and early forties, Alex also studied at the Society of

Arts and Crafts in Detroit, the Art Students League of New York and the Colorado Springs Fine Arts Center.

He summed up the next few years of his life: "When the United States entered World War II, I joined the army and was trained as a combat engineer. Later I volunteered to become a member of Merrill's Marauders. The unit trained in India and we hiked over the Ledo Road into Burma to fight behind the Japanese lines in the jungle. Wounded in combat, I was hospitalized for two years."

The Marauders were the original Special Forces but without helicopters or other high tech. Wounded were evacuated from air strips hand hacked out of the bush. Aided only by pack mules, Marauders walked more than 1,000 miles through extremely dense jungle, attacked the Japanese behind their own lines and won three major battles and twenty-five minor ones. Only 300 of those remaining were considered fit to carry on.

An excerpt from Sergeant Joseph M. Magnotta's journal is succinct:

25 March [1944]: Moved from Ngagahtawng at 0530. Raining marched thru mud, mud and more mud. Carrying ammo and litter cases. Marched to Tigrawmyang. Remained here had hot meal. Message came in and we met our animals here. Saddled up and moved out at 1355. Making forced march on Sharaw. Raining like the dickens. Sent out KCT I&R, BCT I&R and GCT I&R to block trails. Bivouacked here for night and evacuated one patient.

On the morning of 26 March, the remaining ten wounded men, Mills, Minewski, Bushman, O'Neill, McGee, Breedan, Hiscar, Thompson, Norton and Nakada were evacuated by light aircraft.

After release from the hospital, Alex continued his studies perfecting his art in New York, Paris and Colorado and on Monhegan Island, Maine. In 1966, he joined the faculty at SUNY, New Paltz.

On the askart.com website, two former students recalled his impact:

J. J. Fitzsimmons: He was a great teacher; he did much to encourage me. He also showed me a little colored pencil drawing that Picasso sent him to thank him for some bubble gum Minewski somehow arranged for him to get during the war.

David Reina: I knew Professor Minewski in the early seventies, taking many drawing and painting classes over a four year period. He remains to this day the most standout teacher I have ever encountered. He used many, sometimes humorous methods to break us of bad habits. When I teach a class I try to channel his charisma and energy. He often wrote inspirational or humorous sayings on the chalk board and whenever I am getting lazy in my craft I remember this one which he was fond of saying, "Dilettantes are a dime a dozen."

Having been there, Alex was also able to provide support to others wrestling with combat demons. One of them, Larry Winters, paid tribute to Alex's sympathetic understanding of post-Vietnam problems in his book, *The Making and Un-Making of a Marine*.

Prepared by Natalie Minewski and Ray Smith

During his service with the Marauders, Alex earned the Purple Heart, Bronze Star with Oak Leaf Cluster, Combat Infantryman Badge and Ranger tab among other decorations. He died at age sixty-one in 1979 after a long illness. Besides the Art Students League of New York, Alex was a member of the American Institute for the Conservation of History in Artistic Works, the International Institute of the same organization, a recipient of the Purchase Prize of the Detroit Institute of Art, the Tiffany Fellowship, Honorable mention by the American Society of Casein Painters, a participant in the Ball State Drawing Show and a recipient of the State University of New York Research Grant.

THE AMERICAN WOMEN'S VOLUNTARY SERVICES

Natalie Minewski

Natalie in Paris 1953

During the second world war I was a young art student going to Washington Irving High School in Manhattan. As part of the war effort, an organization was formed called "The American Women's Voluntary Services". Since I was enrolled in a commercial art course I was informed of a contest for students to develop a poster encouraging women to donate their time and efforts to the cause.

I made a poster that included a large drawing of a woman's hand, held out, palm up, and the words *"Hand Over Your Leisure Time to AWVS"*.

You can imagine how delighted and surprised I was when it won first prize and was used in the local program. That program bringing women directly into the war effort was a stroke of genius. And that poster was the start of my career as a commercial artist.

When I graduated from high school in 1944 I was in need of a summer job. Since I had some drafting experience I was hired by the U.S. Army to learn how to work on aerial maps of Japan. The location where the maps were being worked on was a rather seedy warehouse in downtown New York. We were being trained to learn aerial map making, presumably for the Air Force bombing missions in Japan. We used detailed maps of small Japanese cities, showing residential areas, commercial areas, and even red light districts where the brothels were located. A group of Japanese Americans were working on other maps in a separate part of the building. There was no interaction allowed between the two groups. I worked on some maps of small cities in Japan but, when Hiroshima was bombed, I felt horrified. I dreamt I was responsible for the atom bomb destruction of the people in Hiroshima and Nagasaki. Of course as an apprentice I was not involved in anything of that nature.

In 1953 I was living in Paris. My first husband, who had just graduated from the Sorbonne on the GI Bill, and I wanted to live in Europe for a while. I was hired by the U.S. Army to make posters for Special Services, informing soldiers stationed at Orly Air Base of the activities available on the base. The job did not pay much money but it was great living as a 'starving artist' in Paris at that time. Eventually my husband got a job working as a civilian personnel writer for NATO and we moved to the army headquarters at La Rochelle. There I was employed as a GS4 Illustrator for NATO, doing maps of supply lines (in case of an attack by Russia?), and large isometric drawings of all the ten NATO bases in France. It was quite an experience! Headquarters was later relocated to Poitiers and we moved there.

My favorite story is the time I completed a "supply line" map and brought it into the colonel's office, as I was instructed to do. Of course I was cleared for "secret", as these were supposed to be important documents. I went back to my office and then, glancing at the material I had been given, realized I had made a mistake. I immediately returned to the colonel's office and asked, "May I have that back? I need to correct something." He replied. "Oh no, *you* can't see that. I just stamped it Top Secret!!" I wonder where the supplies went.

Natalie graduated from Cooper Union Art School in New York City. She lived in Europe for much of the 1950's. She came to New Paltz in 1967 and taught at SUNY New Paltz from 1980-83. Among interesting jobs in New York City, Natalie was a display designer for Helena Rubenstein and a children's book designer at Harper & Row. Natalie is presently involved in the art world in New Paltz and is teaching classes at Lifetime Learning Institute and the local arts community. She moved to Woodland Pond in 2010.

HOME FRONT EXPERIENCES

Addie Reynolds

My dad was an air raid warden. I was about eight or nine years old and the practice "attacks" terrified me. When the sirens sounded homes were darkened, and shades and curtains were closed so light would not be detected if we were attacked. My father grabbed his helmet and searchlight and went to his position in the streets of little old New Paltz. For many years after the war I had dreams in which the Nazis came and stole me away.

We were trained to identify German planes. The charts that we used for identification were black silhouettes on white paper. For years after the war my heart sank when a plane flew over us. Other war efforts involved ordinary citizens, such as saving foil from gum wrappers. I had to separate the paper from the foil. I remember gas rationing; a family had a coupon for so much gas in a designated time. Many days we did not have enough gas for the car. We stayed home a lot.

If war had any good effect, it was the pulling together of everyone to protect us. Women worked in factories as men went to war.

War posters were a part of everyday life, and the patriotic songs were truly felt by all. Pearl Harbor struck horror in everyone, followed by Bataan and the death march. A family friend was on that march and I can still see that young man when he arrived home after much treatment and care. He was skin and bones. It was a horror for me to see him so emaciated—but happily alive.

I was born in New Rochelle, NY on March 1, 1932. My family moved to New Paltz in 1934, where my father opened a pharmacy. I went through the New Paltz school system, ending my high school education at the present middle school. In 1951 I entered Fordham University School of Pharmacy, graduating in 1955.

I was married in 1960, raised three sons and have eight grandchildren. I retired after 55 years of practicing pharmacy in the Hudson Valley area. I entered Woodland Pond in 2009.

A WHITE OFFICER IN A COLORED COMPANY

Joseph A. Rice

Joe with Sergeant and friend

Joe Rice enlisted as a private in the U. S. Army in May 1943 and was discharged as a first lieutenant in August 1946. Twenty months of that time he served in the Pacific as an officer in the Engineers with a company of black troops. The armed services were not integrated until President Truman's Executive Order in 1948. It took another six years before the last all black unit was disbanded.

The following was excerpted from his many letters to his parents from the Philippines and later from Japan with the army of occupation. His company had a fleet of dump trucks hauling debris in Manila and later helping build an airfield ninety miles from Tokyo.

18 and 30 March 1945

I've been assigned to what ought to be a motor officer's dream. Lots and lots of trucks… A dump truck company doesn't sound the least bit romantic, but don't you think for a moment that a company of this sort doesn't have a place in this war. My gosh, we're working all the time… Our company is colored but they're a darn good bunch of boys. Everyone is nice to talk to…

14 April 1945

I want to tell you about Friday the thirteenth. That was quite a day… First was the news of President Roosevelt's death. That's quite a shock considering especially that Truman is now the president. Maybe he has something on the ball and is a dark horse or something, but one thing sure, he isn't like Roosevelt…

[Later that day out in a Jeep with his supply sergeant]

We had a little run in with an MP. He waved us across an intersection and then blew us down… These guys don't like colored drivers and they like to snag them on something. I stepped out and I laced into him. I didn't think I could do it but by golly I do it for my boys.

Today was a very red letter day because we got some States-side apples. I haven't seen any of those since the boat. More for this red letter day: I saw General MacArthur today with his five stars all in a circle. We passed him on the road – we in our dirty jeep and he in his Cadillac. He looks just like his pictures…

1 January 1946

I supposed you have guessed by this time I am in Japan… On land, the Japs were all over the waterfront and in everyone's way. They were like

Filipinos with clothes on… all the children would run out and holler at you when you passed. All had smiles on their faces and some would even hold up the "V" for Victory sign with their fingers. It was very funny. I expected to see a thoroughly squelched people. Sitting back in the States or in Manila or someplace like that one can really hate these Japanese. I mean all of them. But here where one has to live with them and see how they live it's hard to treat them as anything but fellow men and women. That's the American way, though…

21 January 1946

I am what you may call an "occupation troop"… This isn't a particularly enjoyable life… The Army is in an in between stage. During the war everybody was working hard and the outfits were really "on the ball." but now nobody cares about anything. The men just live for the time that they will be eligible to go home… There is a general let down in efficiency that's really noticeable. We officers have all the power needed to punish offenses but who's going to be the cause of a man not going home?

The first sergeant is getting to be a tough man. A good first sergeant, especially in a colored outfit, is the back bone of the organization. Sgt. Miller, first sergeant of the 771st when I arrived, ruled without question by his overwhelming personality.

4 July 1946

This morning I was vaccinated for the fourth time. I've been counting up all the shots I've had. The total is thirty: typhoid, typhus, tetanus, cholera, bubonic plague, influenza, encephalitis. If I could get a shot for athlete's foot, I'd be all set. I'm sorry if I said anything to make you believe that I was going to make a career out of the Army. I'm not even thinking of it. The colonel was trying to get me to volunteer for another year or so. I can't see it and I've told him so. About coming home, rumor has it that I will go to the Depot on the 20th of July. I guess it will be well into August before I get home…

[Joe was home on August 13, 1946 and was back in college three weeks later.]

Originally from Cranford, NJ, Joe and Kay Rice moved to Woodland Pond from Chappaqua, NY. Joe had retired as a corporate executive in 1988. He enjoys the piano, reading history and biography and sculling. He's visited fifty-seven countries – all on business.

Sketch by a street artist in Japan

WHAT IS A SHIPFITTER?

Alvin (Al) Rogerson

Al (see arrow)

As a Shipfitter 3rd Class (SF 3/C) on the *USS Uvalde* (AKA-88) in April 1945, I had many duties. A shipfitter handles shipboard activities including construction and repair (C&R) ranging from the uppermost mast down through the bowels of the ship to the shaft alley propulsive forces that turn the ship's "screws," regulating movement of the ship.

In wartime there are duties involving safety of the ship and advancing the conflict involved. I was on an AKA (Attack Cargo Auxiliary) ship in the South, Central, and Northern Pacific Ocean during World War ll. Our ship had sixteen invasion boats (Higgins Boats) and ten LCMs (Landing Craft Mechanized) that transport tanks or trucks for island invasion activities. The boat crew of ninety members transported troops and supplies to land areas.

During the April 1945 Okinawa Island campaign south of Japan our boats and crew members stayed with the landed troops rather than return to the ship. As a result the ship's total crew was vastly reduced. The remaining crew on board had to assume various other duties. For some reason I was now assigned helmsman activities, steering the four hundred fifty foot ship. Because of Japanese air attacks we and many of the ships in the area were instructed to evacuate the harbor, which was manually fogged by machine generators to prevent detection by enemy aircraft.

I was on the wheel steering the ship under direct orders of the Officer of the Deck (OOD), to follow his precise directions. This I did for approximately fifteen minutes. My C&R division officer manned the port wing of the ship as Assistant OOD to help in observation of ships ahead of us in the fogbank. I maintained position as directed for another five minutes, when the portside Assistant OOD shouted to me to directly alter the course of the ship to starboard. The OOD on the starboard side directed me to maintain "steady on course". The Assistant OOD obviously had better vision (and apparent know-how) of ships ahead and knowingly felt we were on a collision course. With the OOD's directive I had to comply with his command. Upon hearing this the Assistant OOD on the port side dashed into the cabin area and wrenched the wheel from me, directing me to also pull hard to the starboard (countermanding order of the OOD), thus avoiding collision possibility to a ship some seventy-five to one hundred yards ahead. The Assistant OOD was furious at the OOD who showed poor judgment of the potential situation. Quite an experience for me, to be a pawn and obey direct orders thus compelling the Assistant OOD to take direct action to avert a dangerous situation. Needless to say I, a nineteen-year-old, was greatly upset.

The Assistant OOD was given a commendation for positive action. The

OOD was reprimanded by the ship's captain for poor judgment and so cited. I was glad that within the hour I was relieved of the wheel. ...Just an example of a duty I, as shipfitter, had to perform!

Al has degrees from Temple University 1950 and NYU 1956. He was married in 1953, had seven children, moved and worked in four different states. He was a school teacher for 21 years and also employed at hospital and rehab centers. He also had 16 years of senior and masters swim competition in Florida, and lost his home in the 2004 hurricane.

LUCKY ME

Julius Sippen

Julius and his first wife

I guess I was just plain lucky to have survived when thousands died. I had graduated as an Agriculture student, dealing with cows in Animal Husbandry. I was drafted into the Army early in 1941. After basic training I was assigned to the Veterinary Hospital to help care for the horses of the 102nd New Jersey National Guard, a cavalry outfit. (After all, I had been an "Ag" student!) After December 7, 1941 when bombs dropped on

Pearl Harbor, war was declared. Those horses were replaced by tanks.

Our division was placed on alert. We were to be shipped to the European front. I became engaged to a young woman I had met while in training in Columbia, S.C. When my division was ordered overseas she joined the Women's Auxiliary Army Corps (WAACs) and requested to be shipped to Europe also. However, a handful of us men were transferred to Camp Shelby in Mississippi as cadre to form a new infantry division. So she ended up at an airfield base in England and I landed in Mississippi!

The new division was in intensive training. We were shipping out recruits with only eight weeks of basic training because of the dire need for replacements for the Battle of the Bulge. I was working as a medic. All I remember is giving shots in the butt for syphilis! By 1944 I was looking for a change so I applied for Officer's Training. After three months I became a second lieutenant in the Medical Administrative Corps.

Upon graduation 500 of us, second lieutenants through captains, were ordered to the replacement depot at Scofield Barracks on the island of Oahu in Hawaii. This was at the time of the Battle of Iwo Jima. Three days after our arrival we were ordered to depart for Iwo Jima. However, thirteen men were pulled out of the group and assigned to units on Oahu. I was one of the thirteen! Some of my best buddies died on Iwo Jima.

To make things more ridiculous I was assigned to a small outfit in Honolulu that had the responsibility for Mosquito Control and Restaurant Inspection in the city of Honolulu. I spent a great eight to nine months on Oahu before the war ended, and I was discharged at the end of 1945. I swear I did NOT know anybody in the War Department who was looking out for me!

After I was discharged I married my fiancée. We bought a gift shop in Kingston and lived on Lucas Avenue. There we brought up our three children.

I later became an organizer for the International Ladies' Garment Workers Union for a couple of years, trying to maintain and improve wages, working conditions and safety in ladies' garment factories. I then became the ILGWU Manager for the Hudson Valley area including Columbia, Ulster, Dutchess, and Orange Counties (approximately 45 small clothing manufacturers). Beginning in the middle 70s, these small garment businesses were in difficulty because so much of the work was being shipped overseas by the big corporations. They couldn't compete with products made by children, prisoners, and underpaid workers, with no safety or environmental safeguards, in South and Central America and in Asia. They were forced out of business, and their workers became unemployed. I retired early at 65 because the industry had disappeared from the area.

When my wife died in 1982 I moved to Fishkill. Friends introduced me to Lucille Weinstat in 1984. She joined me in Fishkill in 1985. As she was still working and I was retired, I took over the shopping and cooking until her retirement in 1993.

Interviewed by Lucille Weinstat

PEOPLE GOING CRAZY

Robert Sofer

The job of the Persian Gulf Command (PGC, also called "People Going Crazy") was to deliver American supplies through Iran to the Russians as fast as possible. It helped earn this country precious time to prepare for our invasion of Europe, and saved an incalculable number of American lives. It also assisted in the destruction of a large part of the German army. My arrival was a little later in the war, as I was stateside for quite awhile.

I was a Tech Sergeant, sent to Iran as a medic to provide pharmacy service to the troops. (I believe I also filled prescriptions for the Shah.) We were on the ship to the Persian Gulf for sixty days, as the ship had to zigzag and take evasive action to avoid submarines. During that time no mail went out. My wife thought I was dead. On the ship there were several hundred colored troops. They were kept separate. A couple of white soldiers tried to block them from using the communal bathroom, but all was settled quickly and well. There was also a lot of sea-sickness going over.

The temperature in the Persian Gulf was usually 150 degrees. Sometimes it went up to 189. It was a desert area. The locals used to say, referring to the American soldiers, "In July flies die. In August Johnny dies." I spent a few months there.

Then the pharmacist in Teheran had a terrible accident in the hospital lab. He spilled alcohol on himself near an open fire, and was burned to death. I was sent to replace him. I supervised three other men in the hospital pharmacy. Teheran was beautiful, with a temperate climate. The views of the snow capped mountains were wonderful.

One time I was granted a three day leave to go to Hamedan on a pilgrimage to the Tomb of Queen Esther in celebration of the Purim Festival. We were ten men, but we were extremely fortunate to have Captain Cyrus Gordon with us. He was only thirty years old, but an authority on Cuneiform languages, a professor of Assyriology, an historian and an archeologist! He was also a regular guy and one of the best joke tellers I ever met. Jews cherish the story of Queen Esther for the message of faith and hope that it conveys. This can only be appreciated by one who has seen the expressions of faith and hope on the faces of those Persian Jews who flocked to the tomb to listen to the Megillah. Men and women spent the day fasting, praying and sitting so they could be assured of listening to the tale. Purim to them is the greatest of holidays and was celebrated for three days.

When I heard we were being sent home at the end of the war, I couldn't wait to board the ship to get back to my darling wife. Altogether, I served overseas for one and a half years, mostly at the station hospital in Teheran.

Bob spent most of his life in and around New York City, first in the boroughs of Manhattan and The Bronx, then in the suburbs of Yonkers and Bronxville. He and his wife, Lynn, moved to Woodland Pond in 2011; sadly she died shortly after their arrival.

Bob was a pharmacist who practiced his profession until he retired in 2005. At the time his shop was in the Bronx and his home was in Bronxville, a reasonable commute away. He was able to get away from his pharmacy to visit Israel, Italy and elsewhere in Europe. Bob has two sons and two grandchildren.

Interviewer: Lucille Weinstat

OPPONENTS IN WAR—FRIENDS IN PEACE

Lydia Stenzel

Eric Topp

"Red" Ramage

During the 1940s an art school classmate would invite me to parties at the Portsmouth (NH) Naval Shipyard. The young men we met were undergoing intensive training to be submarine commanders.

On weekends the trainees roared with laughter as they retold each other's mistakes from the previous week – "Who rammed the base of the bridge?" and "Who'd take his sub down with the periscope still up??" To further gales of laughter everyone would then toast "Red" Ramage, the American submarine ace and Congressional Medal of Honor winner and then they'd smash their glasses in the fireplace!

Many years later, at the end of the 1970s, my husband and I met a lovely German, Inge Thompson. Inge was the wife of a University of Texas, Dallas, faculty friend. She also turned out to be the step-daughter of Eric Topp, recipient of the World War II German government's Knights Cross with Oak Leaves and Crossed Swords, and an equally renowned submarine commander.

Most interestingly, apparently Ramage and Topp had known of each other, and in the time after the war had become fellow NATO officers in Norfolk, VA, <u>and</u> friends! By the time each retired from their respective naval services, they had become Rear Admiral Eric Topp and Vice Admiral Lawson P. Ramage.

How unbelievable it is that this could happen!! But it really did, and it was a marvel.

As widely traveled as the commanders were in their own ways, Lydia is too. As early as 1944, while working on a summer job with Harvard's Peabody Museum she was offered (but declined) a place on Junius Bird's anthropological expedition to Chile sponsored by the Museum of Natural History in New York. Ten years later, and a graduate of Massachusetts Art, in Drawing and Painting, she was offered an assignment to cover the spring fashion collections in Paris, France, by the New York Daily News. *Rather than go to Paris, though, she instead married her husband, Peter, and set off on an eleven year trip through Nigeria, Ghana and the Netherlands. Returning to Chappaqua, NY, with their four children in 1965, they stayed for eight years before heading out for further adventures in Sumatra, Indonesia. Following their return, they lived in Dallas, TX, for many years before returning to Lydia's home town, Plymouth, MA. Since August 2011, Lydia and Peter have been residents of Woodland Pond.*

FROM NEW GUINEA TO TOKYO

Peter Stenzel

New Guinea 1944

I didn't dream I would be bobbing around in the Pacific Ocean in a life jacket, fully clothed. But to begin at the beginning, when I started out I was a junior in college. I saw the troops marching through, and I didn't want to be in college anymore. I had started out in chemical engineering but it was too much for me at that time. I enlisted in the army and was later assigned to the Fifth Air Force. After Basic Training, they put me in Officer's Candidate School (OCS). (Because I had two years of chemistry, they thought I could be useful in chemical warfare.) When I graduated I was a "Ninety Day Wonder"- a Second Lieutenant.

Well, I wasn't a pilot or in chemical warfare. I was refueling fighter planes, first in New Guinea on the island of Biak. The Pacific was beautiful, with blue skies, lovely beaches and palm trees. We had dug ditches on the beach covered by palm tree trunks and bamboo for camouflage. When the call went out that enemy planes were incoming we all went down into the holes while we were being bombed. The bombers concentrated on the air strip so none of us were hurt.

I was then sent to Leyte in the Philippines. The Naval Construction Battalions (Seabees) had built an airstrip on the shore of Leyte Island, but it was too small. The Japanese fleet was moving south toward the Philippines, and a larger air strip was needed. Mindoro was a big flat island and, because it was agricultural, it was more easily converted to an air base without knocking down too many trees. So we were on our way to Mindoro.

It was a beautiful morning on the Pacific. Suddenly our Landing Ship Tank (LST) was attacked by a kamikaze (suicide) plane. I saw this kamikaze pilot heading right for our boat. The plane had those circles painted on it. I couldn't see much as I ran around to the other side. The plane hit our ship in the midsection and blew up. There were a lot of drums of 100 octane gasoline on the deck which caught fire, and there was no way that the ship could have been saved. We were given orders to go over the side. We grabbed life jackets and lowered ourselves to the water on ropes. We watched as the ship, with the plane and its pilot went down in flames. We floated and bobbed around for a while in the warm Pacific. "I hope there are no sharks," I thought. After a couple of hours we were picked up by the Australian navy.

We did get to Mindoro finally. I was later assigned to a big airbase on Okinawa. One day we were warned that a typhoon was coming but they didn't tell us to dismantle our tents. I was in my tent trying to get a night's sleep. For a while I tried mightily to hold the tent down but it was of no use. All the tents were blown over and shredded by the storm. We were drenched, lying there. Eventually the storm blew over. Luckily we were near the beach, and there was no flying debris. The palm trees just bent over but weren't uprooted. After the Japanese surrender I convinced my commanding officer that the base in Tokyo needed a certain piece of refueling equipment. The train ride was interesting. I was 6'6" and the Japanese were incredibly short. They tried not to stare. While I was walking around Tokyo I was invited into a woman's home for tea. She was alone and spoke no English, but she kept bowing profusely. I nodded back a lot, and somehow we understood each other. The tea was good.

Later I looked for a famous hotel in Tokyo which I had heard of, the Dai-Ichi Hotel. I was surprised to find some of my buddies there. I left the piece of equipment at the air force base but no one was there to accept it. I looked around for souvenirs of the Japanese air force which had been there. I found a poster of a US bomber with diagrams of where to fire on it. I also found an abacus which I later traded for a soft kimono to give to my mom when I got home.

Peter returned to college on the GI Bill and finished his law degree at the University of Virginia. He wanted to go back overseas so took a job with Mobil Oil. He was sent to Cairo, then to Cypress, and then to the new state of Israel. From there he traveled for many years to Asia and Africa.

Interviewer: Lucille Weinstat

HOME FRONT IN THE BRONX

Lucille Weinstat

Pelham Bay 1943

It was wartime. Cousin Elton was coming for dinner. He was my favorite cousin, AND in the Air Force! As a young teenager, this was so-o-o-glamorous. Mom was in the kitchen, rubbing the chicken with onions and paprika. We kids set up the table in the living room and put the chairs around. Soon the house filled with the delicious odors of the roasts. Later we all sat around the table - Eltie in his crisp uniform, my three sisters and I, Mom at the foot of the table (near the kitchen, of course) and Pop at the head. The food was delicious.

"Tell us about the Air Force," we pleaded. "I wanted to be a pilot," he said, "but I was just too short! So they made me a bombardier. It's all pretty new to me."

While eating dessert we started singing. We sang "The Peat Bog Soldiers" (a song written by prisoners in a Nazi concentration camp in 1933), "Viva La Quince Brigada" (from the Spanish Civil War), "Hold On" ("Hold on Winston C., Hold on Franklin D., Hold on Chiang Kai-shek, Hold on Joseph Stalin...."), "Solidarity" (the old union song), "Tumbalalaika" (a Yiddish love song), "Red River Valley", "Clementine", and lots more. Eltie joined in enthusiastically. We all continued singing in the kitchen while we cleaned up.

That was a time when the whole country seemed to be pulling together regardless of party or beliefs. (Well, maybe not the neighbors upstairs who used to belong to the German-American Bund, an American Nazi organization) Pop was an air raid warden with a very impressive helmet. My twin and I collected silk stockings for parachutes, and aluminum foil which we rolled into big balls for the war effort. We lived in an apartment building in New York City, and couldn't have a Victory Garden. However, Harriet and Mitzi went Farming for Victory. They picked apples and dug onions in the Hudson Valley during the summer. We had blackout shades on the windows, and people who owned automobiles had the top half of their headlights painted silver so enemy airplanes wouldn't see them. It looked as if the cars had drooping eyelids. My big sister Beulah commuted to a DuPont defense plant in New Jersey where she packed powder into bullet casings.

When my next biggest sister Mitzi got old enough, she joined the WACs. She was stationed at Montgomery Airfield in Alabama. She did orientation and also worked as a lifeguard for American and foreign airmen there for Rest and Rehabilitation (R&R). Mom had to juggle food stamps and rationing when she got home from work. But for me it was an exciting, romantic time. But then, I was a teenager.

One day we received a letter from Elton on the thin onion-skin paper the soldiers were using. It came with a 45 rpm disc. He had recorded himself singing "I'm gonna buy a Paper Doll that I can call my own...." a popular song of the time. He had a sweet voice. The letter had been severely edited by the censor, so we really didn't know where he was or what he was doing. However, we were thrilled to get it.

Just after ceasefire in Asia was announced, Elton was killed when his plane went down over the "Hump" in Burma.

Lucille's mom, Lucille, sister Beulah and twin sister Harriet

Lucille studied voice at the High School of Music and Art, then received her BA in Occupational Therapy and MA in Rehabilitation Counseling. She worked as a rehabilitation counselor, later as an occupational therapist until her children were born, and returned to work when her younger daughter turned four. She also worked as an OT in Home Care after retiring. Her last full time job was for the state office of Vocational and Educational Services for the Disabled in Poughkeepsie.

Lucille also worked as a singer professionally for a few years, singing in the NY Choral Society and several other choruses over the years. She studied art and photography in various schools, one course at a time, and has had several solo shows. She studied ecology, birds and wildflower botany on her own with the aid of courses at the New York Museum of Natural History, and trained as a trail guide in the Northern Everglades (Fish and Wildlife Service) after she retired.

Lucille's first husband died in 1982. In 1984 she was introduced to Julius Sippen by the owner of a hotel where her husband and she had vacationed. "Julie" had been

widowed in 1982 also. They decided to live together and she moved to the Hudson Valley in 1985. Together they have six grandkids and three great grandchildren

GROWING UP DURING THE WAR

Carl Yettru

Navy 1945-46

In our small upstate New York town there was not much to make us– or me– aware of the impending conflict raging in Europe, and what invisible forces were about to bring the U.S. into the war. It became clear to us one Sunday when we heard that Pearl Harbor had undergone a surprise attack. All of us were numb and speechless; life in this village was about to change.

Rationing was difficult to accept not only for the annoyingly precise calculation that it required but also because my dad, a local minister, was put in charge by the Office of Price Administration (OPA) of enforcing these price regulations. It did not make him the most popular man in town– particularly with the store owners, who were given the immensely frustrating job of sorting things out. The gasoline rationing, although necessary, caused a great deal of anxiety and finger pointing.

Soon civilian defense measures were put in place. My dad was one of many put on patrol to ensure the blackout regulations were in compliance. As a high school student I had the task of riding my bike carrying messages from one post to another during blackouts. Of course we were simply saying to ourselves, "Why are we so careful? The enemy planes are not going to bomb this tiny place!" Did we realize that it was all part of a bigger plan? We were given lessons in school in identifying friendly and enemy planes, and we became quite good at it.

Since all kinds of scrap metal were needed for the war effort, we were given time from school to go about picking it up, particularly from the many farmers. I have often wondered how that beat-up old Model A Ford pickup, lent to us by a local farmer, ever stood up with all the stuff we carried. We also helped local farmers by digging potatoes, a painful job. Even more painful was seeing many blue stars in windows replaced by gold stars, indicating that a son or brother had given his full sacrifice. This certainly brought the grim reality of war to this small town.

I attended a small college in northern Georgia for a year. Memories of red clay, a quieter and slower pace, friendly faces and local scenery still linger with me. However, the one event that is deeply etched is witnessing the lonesome train that carried President Roosevelt's casket northward. I hitched a ride on that April day to nearby Cornelia, Georgia, where a large but hushed crowd gathered along the tracks. The people stood patiently and quietly despite the delay of the train. One could sense the arrival as the closer watchers became respectfully silent. As the train passed the mournful silence was broken only by the clacking and whirling of the locomotive and cars slowly huffing through. Even though I had been merely curious, I was totally pulled into the momentous importance of what I had experienced.

The welcome victory in Europe was followed in August, 1945 by the surrender of Japan, leading to celebrations throughout the country. Even though the war was over I was drafted and allowed my choice of services.

I chose the navy. After an uneventful ten-month stint in Camp Peary, Virginia, I was discharged, providing me the opportunity of the GI Bill. I attended Utica College and graduated in 1949. Things were brewing in Korea and when conflict broke out I was drafted again. (They must like me!) After basic training the army sent me to radio school, then to a communications company which, fortunately, was shipped to Germany—not Korea!

Army 1950-52

I was born in Albany, NY on June 27, 1927, to Eloise O. Yettru, wife of Rev. Carl H. Yettru. After a brief stay in Sharon Springs, NY, we moved to New Ulm, MN and then back to New York to Roscoe, NY. Since two churches in Roscoe were merging, my dad was let go in deference to the other pastor. That led to our moving to Lew Beach, N Y where my dad had a small church. Unaware of the problems that my parents had to face, I thoroughly enjoyed being there in that small, rural village, exploring and doing chores around the house. Too soon for me but not for my parents, who dealt with neither indoor plumbing nor electricity, we moved to Bridgewater, NY.

It was in this farming community that we experienced the war years, doing what we could in school and in the town to help in the war effort. After a college year in Georgia I was drafted, choosing the Navy where I spent only ten months, since World War II had ended. Through the GI Bill I attended and graduated from Utica College in 1949. The draft board must have liked me because when the Korean Conflict broke out in 1950, they called me again--this time to the Army. I served two years and ended up as a slow speed radio operator, which helped me become an amateur radio operator later in civilian life.

I was fortunate to get a job as a Youth Secretary in the Tarrytown YMCA. I had not realized how really fortunate I was because it was through meetings and conferences with other Y workers that I met a beautiful young lady who later became my wife! I soon realized that I had to use my GI Bill or lose the benefits. Consequently, I resigned from the Y and enrolled in Teachers College, Columbia University, from which I later received my Masters Degree. I started teaching in Dobbs Ferry, NY in September of 1955 and on October 1 I was blessed to marry Vivian! Five years later we moved to Cornwall, NY to escape the high taxes - HA! They followed us up the river. I taught in Newburgh and in 1991 I retired. Now we are residing very comfortably in Woodland Pond New Paltz.

Made in the USA
Charleston, SC
29 July 2013